George Wallis

The Royal House of Tudor: A series of biographical sketches

Illustrated with a series of portraits

George Wallis

The Royal House of Tudor: A series of biographical sketches
Illustrated with a series of portraits

ISBN/EAN: 9783337103118

Printed in Europe, USA, Canada, Australia, Japan

Cover: Foto ©Thomas Meinert / pixelio.de

More available books at **www.hansebooks.com**

THE ROYAL HOUSE OF TUDOR.

THE

Royal House of Tudor.

A SERIES OF BIOGRAPHICAL SKETCHES

BY GEORGE WALLIS,

KEEPER OF THE ART DIVISION, SOUTH
KENSINGTON MUSEUM.

ILLUSTRATED WITH A SERIES OF PORTRAITS EXECUTED
FROM AUTHENTIC CONTEMPORARY WORKS, FOR
THE PRINCE'S CHAMBER, IN THE NEW
PALACE AT WESTMINSTER

BY RICHARD BURCHETT,

HEAD MASTER OF THE NATIONAL ART TRAINING SCHOOL,
SOUTH KENSINGTON.

REDUCED FROM PHOTOGRAPHS TAKEN FROM THE ORIGINALS

BY C. THURSTON THOMPSON.

LONDON·
CUNDALL AND FLEMING, 168, NEW BOND STREET
SAMPSON LOW, SON, & MARSTON, LUDGATE HILL.
1866.

Contents.

Preface.

HE biographical sketches which accompany the portraits forming the leading features of this volume were originally written for the instruction of my own children, and as historical illustrations of the larger series of photographs from the paintings in the Prince's Chamber, at the New Palace of Westminster, issued by the Science and Art Department* in 1860.

The notices of the more prominent personages in English history, such as Henry VII, Henry VIII, Edward VI, Queen Elizabeth, and one or two others, have been purposely kept as brief as possible, consistent with giving the leading facts in the career of each; because more detailed information is easily accessible in ordinary histories. Those, however, of the lesser known individuals, especially in Scottish history, have been comparatively extended, for the opposite reason. This will account for the variation in length of the biographical sketches, which do not always correspond in extent to the historical importance of the subjects of them.

* Now published by Messrs. Cundall & Co, 168, New Bond Street.

The labour has been one of more reading than writing; but the end kept in view has been to render the histories acceptable and instructive to the young of both sexes, whilst avoiding strong party or sectarian bias in giving the leading incidents of an age painfully characterized by both.

GEORGE WALLIS.

October, 1865.

Introductory Notice of the Decorations of the Prince's Chamber, New Palace of Westminster.

HE original paintings from which the photographs forming the illustrations of this volume were taken, form part of the decorations of the Prince's Chamber, in the New Palace at Westminster.

This apartment, which is practically the antechamber to the House of Peers, was originally called the Royal Antechamber; but the designation was changed to that of the Prince's Chamber in consequence of there having been a corresponding room in the Old Houses of Parliament.

The decorations of this chamber are part of the system adopted in the ornamentation and artistic embellishment of the New Palace of the Legislature. This has opened a field for the revival of certain arts in England which had been too long neglected. Amongst them may be named fresco painting, stained glass, the higher class of metal work as applied to architectural decoration, wood carving, &c, whilst amongst the newer processes resulting from the progress of science, painting with water-glass medium, and on incised millboards or paper panels, in imitation of the ancient decorative leather hangings, have been tried with great success.

The twenty-eight portraits of the Tudor Family, now reproduced by photography, are executed in the latter manner. Each panel is formed of stout millboard, saturated so completely with oil as to be practically impervious to damp—the uncompromising foe and destroyer of the ancient leather hangings of the Middle Ages. In each subject, the details of the ornamentation which surrounds the figure is carefully incised in the surface of the panel, and then the whole is gilt and painted, the effect being essentially architectonic and ornamental, rather than pictorial.

It was to the judgment and taste, in other words to the accurate perception of fitness in art matters, of His Royal Highness the late Prince Consort, we owe the scheme of the decorations of this apartment, now so appropriately named.

The portraits of the principal members of the Royal House of Tudor occupy the twenty-eight compartments into which the upper portions of the wall are divided, at a suitable height above the doors and fire-places. It was at first intended to have filled the six large spaces or compartments above them with tapestries, taken wholly or in part from the tapestries representing the defeat of the Spanish Armada, originally used as decorations in the old House of Peers. But although this was abandoned, the whole of the decorations have reference to the Tudor era, except the great marble group by John Gibson, R.A., representing Her Majesty Queen Victoria, supported by the figures of Justice and Clemency.

This group is opposite the entrance from the Royal Gallery, and on each side of it are doors giving access to the House of Lords. A richly decorated fire-place occupies the centre of each end of the apartment. Over the one on the right is a bas-relief in bronze representing " The Field of the Cloth of Gold." Over that on the left is a similar work, " The Visit of Charles V. to Henry VIII." These reliefs, as also those to be named, were designed and modelled by Mr. William Theed.

In the three compartments to the right of the first named fire-place, are bas-reliefs of " Drake spreading his Cloak as a Carpet for Queen Elizabeth," " Queen Elizabeth Knighting Drake," and " The Death of Sir Philip Sydney," the second named being the centre panel. Corresponding to them, and on the other side of the entrance from the Royal Gallery, are the subjects, " Mary Queen of Scots looking back to France," " The Escape of Mary Queen of Scots," and " The Murder of Rizzio," " The Escape of Mary " filling the centre compartment.

In the panels at the upper part of the side of the door, to the left of the marble group, are the subjects, " Edward VI. granting a Charter to Christ's Hospital," and " Lady Jane Grey at her Studies." At the side of the other door, the subjects filling the compartments are, " Sebastian Cabot before Henry VIII," and " Katherine of Arragon pleading."

It will thus be seen, as already stated, that these bas-reliefs have direct relation to events in the career of the personages whose portraits form the chief decorations of the apartment.

The details of the ornamentation of the ceiling, upper walls, and fire-places, do not require mention here, as the object of this introductory notice is to explain the general scheme of the historical illustrations in their relation to the portraits.

HENRY VII

Henry VII.

ENRY VII. was the son of Margaret of Lancaster, a grand-daughter of John of Gaunt, Duke of Lancaster. She married Edmund Tudor, Earl of Richmond, usually supposed to be a brother of Henry VI, but in reality his half-brother only; as his mother, Catherine, daughter of Charles VI, King of France, married for her second husband Owen Tudor, a Welch gentleman. Hence the family name of the royal line of Tudor.

He was born at Pembroke Castle in Wales, on 26th of June, 1456. His father died when he was only fifteen weeks old, his mother being little more than thirteen when he was born.

When he was about three years old, his young and widowed mother, then scarcely seventeen, presented him to his great-uncle, Henry VI. The old king is said to have placed his hand on the head of the child, and to have uttered what appeared to the young and fond mother, a solemn prophecy, which she cherished amid all her after vicissitudes :—" This pretty boy will wear the garland in peace for which we so sinfully contend." Margaret Beaufort lived to see her faith in this prediction amply justified.

The early life of Henry of Richmond must have been one of great hardship and vicissitude, as the then reigning family of York persecuted the members of the House of Lancaster, and their adherents, without mercy. This had, no doubt, a great effect upon his character in after-life, in rendering it hard and unrelenting. Richard III. had usurped the throne of his nephew, Edward V, and, as he supposed, effectually secured the crown for himself and his son, a boy of eight years old; when a strong party of nobles, still attached to the House of Lancaster, formed a plot against him with the intention of placing Richmond on the throne, on condition that he married the Princess Elizabeth, daughter of Edward IV. This effort failed, and the Duke of Buckingham, leader of the insurgent party, lost his head. After this formidable conspiracy was suppressed, Richard entered London in triumph, in December, 1483. On 9th of April, 1484, his only child, Edward, died; and this, with other circumstances, again raised the hopes of his opponents. Henry of Richmond, supposed to have been on the Continent, is now generally understood to have been in Wales, where he had many adherents amongst the friends of the Tudor family. After a journey to France, in which he collected a body of English exiles and some French soldiers, he landed at Haverfordwest on 7th of August, 1485.

At first Richard treated this effort with assumed contempt; then finding that he could place little or no reliance on those about him, (for the cruel and unprincipled are always suspicious), he lost all his usual caution, and acting more in desperation than from firm principle, he prepared to meet his enemies in the field. On 22nd of August he marched out of Leicester, encamped at the Abbey of Merivale, and finally fell in the battle of Bosworth Field; leaving Richmond conqueror and king, under the title of Henry VII.

Henry was now thirty years old, of pale complexion, thin, and care-worn, his grave deportment indicating an older man. He had lived amongst plots until he had become suspicious, cold, and designing. By no means of brilliant ability, he made up for his deficiencies by great industry and perseverance. Avarice and an intense hatred of the House of York appear to have been his ruling passions. He had, however, from motives of policy, to bridle one of these, in order to secure the crown to which he had attained, as it became necessary for the future peace of the country, to unite the two rival factions; and to this end he married, in accordance with a previous arrangement, the Princess Elizabeth of York, eldest daughter of Edward IV. and Elizabeth Woodville; but fearing that this marriage might be considered as his only claim to the throne, in the right of his wife, he postponed it until after his own coronation, and would not permit her name to appear in the Act of Parlament for settling the succession.

As may be supposed, Henry did not rest in undisturbed possession of the throne. An attempt was made in 1487 to raise a rebellion, by putting forward Lambert Simnel, the son of a baker at Oxford, as the young Earl of Warwick, whom it was pretended had escaped from the Tower. In Ireland he was actually proclaimed as Edward VI. Henry soon put down his claims in England, by showing the true Earl of Warwick to the people of London. An army, however, was landed in Lancashire from Ireland, and Henry met it at Newark, on 16th of June, 1487, and defeated it. After this, an attempt was made to personate the younger brother of Edward V, so cruelly murdered by Richard III. in the Tower; and a youth named Perkin Warbeck, whose polished manners and well-told story imposed upon many persons, was declared to be the true king of England, under

the title of Richard IV. The Duchess of Burgundy, sister
of the young and unfortunate victims of Richard, first supported Simnel's claim, and then believing, or affecting to
believe, that Perkin Warbeck was the long-lost brother,
received him at her court, and induced James IV. of
Scotland to take up arms for the restoration of the House of
York. The Scots invaded England in October, 1496, and
commenced, as usual, to plunder the people. Warbeck
remonstrated against the barbarity, and this probably helped
to cool the ardour of James. Henry managed to enter into
communication with the Scottish King, and as he had
enough upon his hands in the suppression of an insurrection
of Cornish men, who penetrated as far as Blackheath before
they were met and defeated, he preferred negotiation to war;
and James, detaching himself from Warbeck, who went to
Ireland, returned home, and finally accepted the hand of
Margaret Tudor, eldest daughter of Henry VII, in marriage.

Warbeck subsequently landed at Whitsand Bay, Cornwall,
the refractory Cornish men joining him. After some
fighting he was taken prisoner by the king's troops at the
Abbey of Beauley. Promised his life to get him out of
sanctuary, he was brought to London. After an escape from
the Tower and an appearance on a scaffold at Westminster
to confess his imposture, he was hung at Tyburn, on 23rd
of November, 1499, the Earl of Warwick dying by the axe
on the same day at the Tower.

Undisturbed possession of the crown resulted to Henry.
Henceforth, whilst he gave considerable development to
commerce, he chiefly employed himself in amassing wealth,
which was obtained in the most unscrupulous manner.
Money, plate, jewels, &c, were got together and stored
away in secret apartments in his palace at Richmond.
After the death of Arthur, Prince of Wales, who had

married Katherine of Arragon, so unwilling was he to part
with that princess's dowry, or even lose the half which had
not been paid, that he caused her to be betrothed in marriage
to his second son, Henry, afterwards Henry VIII, although
he was only a boy of eleven years old.

When his queen, Elizabeth of York, died, in 1503, he
wished to marry the Queen Dowager of Naples, under the
impression that she was enormously rich; finding this to
be erroneous, he abandoned his intention.

As his end drew nigh, the ruling spirit of avarice and
penuriousness manifested themselves in many curious forms,
mixed up with much of superstition and fear.

His death took place in his palace at Richmond, on 21st
April, 1509, in the fifty-fourth year of his age, and twenty-
fourth of his reign. He was buried in the magnificent
chapel he had planned and partially constructed, now known
as Henry VII's chapel at Westminister.

He had three sons and four daughters by his marriage with
Elizabeth of York :—Arthur, Prince of Wales, died in his
eighteenth year ; Henry, who succeeded him as Henry VIII;
and Prince Edward, who died when a year old ; Margaret,
who married James IV. of Scotland, and afterwards Douglas,
Earl of Angus ; Mary, married to Louis XII. of France,
and afterwards to Charles Brandon, Duke of Suffolk ; and
two princesses who died in infancy. The children who
attained adult age became the progenitors of the Royal
House of Tudor in its various subsequent phases.

The authorities from which the portrait was painted are
a copy by Remée, from the original, by Holbein, destroyed
by fire in the Palace at Whitehall, and the bronze figure by
Torrigiano, on the tomb of Henry VII's Chapel at West-

Elizabeth of York,

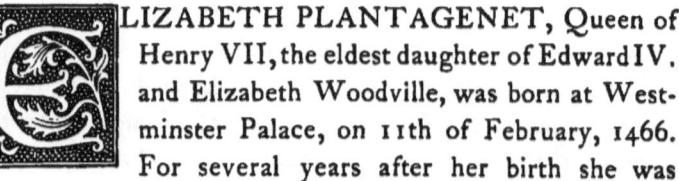

LIZABETH PLANTAGENET, Queen of Henry VII, the eldest daughter of Edward IV. and Elizabeth Woodville, was born at Westminster Palace, on 11th of February, 1466. For several years after her birth she was heiress to the throne of England. On the flight of her father she accompanied her mother and two little sisters when they took sanctuary at Westminster, during the ascendancy of the Lancastrian party, and while in this place of refuge, her eldest brother, Edward, was born. The victorious return of her father again restored prosperity to the House of York, and Elizabeth was subsequently contracted to the dauphin Charles, heir to Louis XI. of France, after that king had agreed to pay tribute to Edward IV. for the French provinces acquired by Henry V. In the agreement Edward undertook to resign to his intended son-in-law, Charles, the Dukedom of Guienne or Aquitaine, with the understanding that this was to be considered as a part of his daughter's dower. From this time she was always addressed as " Madame la Dauphine," and was instructed in the French language, as also in Spanish. This contract was just upon the point of completion, the dresses of the princess are even stated to have been prepared after the most approved French

style of the period, when Louis XI. violated his part of the bond, and proposed to the Duke of Burgundy for his heiress. This insult so enraged King Edward that it is said to have seriously affected his health, and is generally supposed to have accelerated his death.

The events which occurred on the decease of the father led to the mother again seeking sanctuary at Westminster, to avoid the brutal persecution of King Richard III, by whose orders the brothers of Elizabeth, Edward V. and Richard, Duke of York, were destroyed in the Tower of London, in order that he might usurp the crown.

In order, if possible, to meet the rival claims of the Houses of York and Lancaster a marriage between Elizabeth and Henry, Earl of Richmond, afterwards Henry VII, was privately negotiated by the mothers of both. The effect of this contract was to unite certain nobles against Richard. Subsequently this contract was apparently broken off. After the death of the queen of Richard III, Anne of Warwick, who, it is said, "always treated Elizabeth of York as a sister," the mother of the latter consented to her marriage with Richard; but this arrangement was defeated by the princess herself rejecting him; although she was wrongfully charged with having desired the death of Anne, in order that Richard might claim her for his wife.

The rejection of his advances, however, led to her being sent to a northern castle, and kept in close confinement. This is in itself a sufficient contradiction to the calumny uttered against her by violent opponents of the family and her claims to the throne.

The landing of the Earl of Richmond at Haverfordwest, in August, 1485, soon followed by the decisive battle of Bosworth Field, which resulted in the defeat and death of Richard, and the proclamation of Richmond, as Henry VII, led to a change in the condition of the princess; for Richmond, in consideration of the assistance rendered by her party, headed by Lord Stanley, had pledged himself to make her his queen.

Elizabeth, who was a prisoner in the castle of Sheriff Hutton, Yorkshire, was invited to return to London. Henry publicly renewed his engagement with her as a means of finally settling the rival interests of the White and Red Roses, as representing the Houses of York and Lancaster. Jealousy, however, of her claim to the throne, as the eldest surviving child of King Edward IV, caused Henry to postpone the marriage until after his coronation. Elizabeth became his wife on 18th of January, 1486, but was not crowned as Queen until 25th of November, 1488.

Whatever may be said of the penuriousness, political cunning, and worldly scheming of King Henry VII, he was undoubtedly a good and faithful husband; and according to all the evidence brought together, as to the private life of Henry Tudor and his amiable partner, the union was a happy one: for, although beset with many trials and troubles, living as they did in the midst of unscrupulous factions in a loose age, they appear to have found their greatest pleasure in each other's society and that of their children.

Elizabeth of York was surnamed "The Good" by her people. She was beautiful, gentle, and accomplished. Her family misfortunes endeared her mother and sister to her in a remarkable degree, and her devotion to the memory of her murdered brothers was proverbial in her own day. She was the mother of three sons—Arthur, Prince of Wales, who died at the age of seventeen; Prince Henry, afterwards Henry VIII; and Prince Edward, created Duke of Somerset, who died at Hatfield, Hertfordshire, when about one year old; and also four daughters—Margaret, afterwards

Queen of Scotland; Elizabeth, who died at Eltham in her fourth year; Mary, afterwards Queen of Louis XIII. of France; and Katherine, who died in her infancy a short time after the death of the queen, which took place on her birthday, 11th of February, 1502-3, on which day she was thirty-seven years old. She died in the Tower of London, which she had selected as the birth-place of her last child, but was interred in Westminster Abbey with great ceremony. Sir Thomas Moore wrote an elegy upon her death, in which he alludes to the affection which existed between herself, the king, and the children. As no one had better opportunity of judging than he, his statement can certainly be relied on.

Henry's character deteriorated greatly after the queen's death. Her gentle influence had kept him right in many things, and he missed her probably more than he expected.

The authorities for the portrait are a copy by Remée, from the original, by Holbein, destroyed by fire at Whitehall, and the bronze figure by Torrigiano, on the tomb in Henry VII's Chapel at Westminster.

Prince Arthur,

RTHUR, the eldest son of Henry VII. and his queen, Elizabeth of York, was born at the Castle of Winchester, on 20th of September, 1486, and three years afterwards was created Prince of Wales. While still an infant, his diplomatic father negotiated a marriage contract between him and Katherine of Arragon, daughter of Ferdinand and Isabella of Spain.

The education of the prince was very carefully attended to, and he showed considerable ability ; while he was beloved for his amiable and unobtrusive disposition. He corresponded with his betrothed bride in Latin, and one letter, written in 1499, and dated at Ludlow Castle, when he was thirteen years old, was addressed " To the most illustrious and excellent Princess, the Lady Katherine, Princess of Wales, Duchess of Cornwall, and my most entirely beloved spouse." In this epistle he says, " I have read the sweet letters of your highness lately given unto me, from which I easily perceived your most entire love to me. Truly these letters, traced by your own hand, have so delighted me, and made me so cheerful and jocund, that I fancied I beheld your highness, and conversed with and embraced my dearest wife. I cannot tell you what earnest desire I feel to see

your highness, and how vexatious to me is this procrastination about your coming."

In 1501, however, this "procrastination" ceased, and on 17th of August, Katherine embarked at Corunna for England, but was driven back by bad weather to the coast of Old Castile. After recovering from the ill effects of this attempt to cross the sea, which the chroniclers say "occasioned great illness to donna Catalina," the bridal party once more sailed from Corunna on 26th of September, and landed at Plymouth on 2nd of October. Here Katherine was received with great demonstrations. In due course, and after much etiquette, Spanish and English, Prince Arthur met his bride at Dogmersfield, in the presence of his father Henry VII, who caused them to personally plight their troth in confirmation of the betrothal by proxy eleven years previously.

The ceremony was performed on 14th of November, 1501, at Old St. Paul's, Katherine being led there from the Bishop's Palace by Prince Henry, then Duke of York (afterwards her second husband, Henry VIII). Of course there were great rejoicings, a grand banquet at the Bishop's Palace, pageants, processions, masques, and balls. A tilt-yard was established in the open space before Westminster Hall, the river was alive with revellers making their way from the City, in imitation of the bride and bridegroom in their passage from the Bishop's Palace, the day after their marriage, to Baynard's Castle, and thence to Westminster Hall, in which ballets, pageants, and dancing were the order of the day.

To such an extent was this revelry carried, that the frail frame of the prince was visibly affected by the excitement; for he was still but a boy of a few months over sixteen, and his bride was only ten months older, and not, as some historians state, four years his senior.

As Prince and Princess of Wales the young couple were sent to Ludlow Castle, in Shropshire, there to hold a mimic court for the principality. On their way Prince Arthur visited Oxford, and was entertained at Magdalen College; but no mention is made on the records that the princess was with him.

The journey to Ludlow was performed after the usual fashion of those days, Katherine riding in a pillion behind the master of the horse. She was accompanied by eleven ladies on palfreys. The use of a litter borne between two horses relieved the tedium of the journey, as by these means the cavalcade could traverse roads, such as they were, which no wheeled carriage could have got through.

The prince appears never to have properly recovered from the excitement produced by the rejoicings and endless ceremonies of his marriage, for soon after his arrival at Ludlow Castle, he showed symptoms of decline, of which he died on 2nd of April, 1502—and not of the plague, as is sometimes stated—within six months after his union with Katherine, who was thus left a widow among strangers. Prince Arthur was buried with great pomp at Worcester Cathedral, on the right side of the chancel. A beautiful little chapel was subsequently erected over the tomb, from designs by Sir Reginald Bray the eminent statesman.

During the short married life of Arthur and Katherine, there appears to have been none of that familiar intercourse which grows with, as it lives on, affection. They could only converse with each other through the limited medium of Latin, and if the prince's will is to be taken as an evidence of his sentiments towards his Spanish bride, it is clear that, with whatever courtesy he may have treated her, as arising out of a naturally amiable disposition, he really felt no affection for her; since he failed to bequeath to her any of

his personal property, having left the whole of it to his
sister Margaret, the Queen of Scotland.

The only sympathy Katherine appears to have met with
was from her mother-in-law, the good and kind queen,
Elizabeth of York; who, although in great grief at the
sudden loss of her eldest son, the most beloved of all her
children, sent for his virgin widow to London, and provided
as tenderly as circumstances would allow for her convey-
ance there, where she received her with all that a mother's
love could bestow, and placed her at Croydon Palace.

The authority for the portrait is a picture by Mabuse, in
the collection at Hampton Court Palace.

Katherine of Arragon.

HE first queen of King Henry VIII. was the youngest child and fourth daughter of Ferdinand of Arragon and Isabella of Castile, King and Queen of Spain. She was born at Alcala de Henares on 15th of December, 1485. Her infancy was passed in the camp before Grenada, at that time besieged by Ferdinand and Isabella in their efforts to subdue the Moors, and she shared the triumph of her parents on their entry into Grenada. Isabella had the reputation of being the most learned princess of Europe, and she certainly imparted a taste for scholastic pursuits to her daughters. Katherine could read and write Latin at an early age, and always evinced a fondness for study.

While Katherine was yet an infant, Henry VII. proposed an alliance between her and his eldest son, Arthur, Prince of Wales. The Spanish princess was finally guaranteed a dowry of 200,000 crowns, after much diplomacy; and the betrothal took place on 28th of March, 1489, when the Infanta was in her fourth year, and the prince in his third.

In 1501 the Infanta Catalina, for such was her Spanish name, then in her sixteenth year, set out for England. She left the Palace of the Alhambra at Grenada on 21st of May, and landed at Plymouth on 2nd of October, after considerable delays from bad weather and illness.

After much ceremony on the part of both King Henry and the Spaniards, the marriage took place at Old St. Paul's, on 14th of November, 1501.

The young prince's health gave way under the excitement of these merry-makings, and he seems to have fallen into a decline; (although some accounts state that he was seized with the plague,) and died on 2nd of August, 1502. He was interred in Worcester Cathedral.

Very little real affection is said to have existed between Prince Arthur and Katherine; and probably King Henry VII. was aware of this, since he appears to have very soon proposed a union between the girl-widow and his next heir, Henry, now Prince of Wales. No doubt the Spanish dowry had much to do with this, as only one half of it had been paid. A dispensation from the Pope having been obtained, Henry and Katherine were duly betrothed, in spite of the repugnance and remonstrances of the latter. The queen appears to have behaved more kindly to Katherine than any other person, for the king acted as if he considered it quite justifiable to punish his daughter-in-law by semi-starvation in order to compel the payment of the balance of the dowry. Unfortunately Isabella of Castile died about this time, and Ferdinand paid little attention to his daughter's letters imploring him for assistance. Her discipline must have been very severe, and she must have exercised great self-denial, and the suppression of naturally generous feelings, until the death of King Henry VII. in April, 1509.

Prince Henry succeeded to the throne in his nineteenth year, and, in defiance of protests by Warham, Archbishop of Canterbury, his marriage with his brother's widow, Katherine of Arragon, took place on 11th of June, 1509. These protests, however, were very useful when Henry wished to dissolve this union in order to marry Anna Boleyn.

Katherine was in her twenty-fourth year, and King Henry in his nineteenth year, when their marriage took place, and the union appears to have been a happy one tor many years. The queen's advantage in age and experience, her self-denial, love of learning and all the womanly pursuits of the time, had a beneficial influence on the character of the young king. Unfortunately the children of Queen Katherine all died in infancy, except the Princess Mary, afterwards queen, who was the only survivor of five—three sons and two daughters.

In 1511, during Henry's wars with France, Queen Katherine administered the affairs of England, and it was at this period the victory at Flodden Field, so disastrous to the Scots, was gained by the Earl of Surrey.

The evil days of Katherine of Arragon are, however, those by which she is best remembered in English history. Her indomitable courage, her sense of right and justice, her determination not to yield in any degree to the unlawful and degrading wishes of her husband, are all points on which the people of England dwelt with pleasure at the time, and have remembered with satisfaction ever since.

History records the sufferings of Henry's first queen at sufficient length to show her to great advantage as the opponent at once of the King, Cardinal Wolsey, and Dr. (afterwards archbishop) Cranmer. Furious at her resistance to his wishes that the marriage should be dissolved " for the quieting of his conscience," when she refused to refer the matter at issue to four noblemen and four bishops, he practically turned her out of his house: for on 14th of June, 1529, just twenty years after their marriage, he left Windsor Castle, and sent orders that she should leave before he returned. She obeyed, with the expression, "Go where I may, I am his wife; and for him will I pray." From that time the king, and her child, the Princess Mary, were practically dead to her, as she never saw either again.

After a stay at Ware, in Hertfordshire, she went to reside

t Ampthill, from whence she wrote excellent letters to her aughter. In spite of threats aimed at her child, the queen ras unconquered and unconquerable. In 1533 she changed er residence for Brigden, near Huntingdon; and here she egained in some degree her cheerfulness and renewed ealth; which, as might have been expected, had suffered much under the rude shocks to which she had been sub-:cted. If ill-health was her fate in prosperity—and this ras one of the king's excuses for putting her away—it was ot likely to be improved by the treatment she received. All her faithful servants, too, were subjects of the king's ersecution, and various residences, all more or less un-ealthy, were from time to time proposed to her; but at .st she was compelled to settle at Kimbolton Castle, in)ecember, 1534. During the six years which had elapsed nce her separation from the king, although she had defied ·ith comparative impunity, she never forfeited his esteem.

It was at Kimbolton the closing scenes of her life occurred, nd on 7th of January, 1536, she departed, in her fifty-second ear. She was buried at Peterborough Abbey on 26th of anuary; and when, some time after, the king was asked to ·ect some monument to mark the spot in which she lay, e replied that " he would have to her memory one of the noodliest monuments in Christendom;" and he kept his ord by the erection of the Abbey Church of Peterborough . this monument. A small brass plate let into the stone por at the north entrance to the choir now points out the ·tual spot in which the body of Queen Katherine rests. fine ornamental tomb is said to have covered her remains : one period.*

* The first burial-place of Mary Queen of Scots, in which her body y for twenty-five years, was on the opposite side of the choir of Peter

c

Katherine of Arragon was a woman of great ability and varied accomplishments. She was versed in the Flemish, French, and English languages, and wrote well in her native Spanish. She was the principal instructress of her daughter in Latin, and excelled as a needle-woman, and in all the domestic arts followed by the ladies of her time. Her virtuous life, her piety, and consistency, above all her great charity and consideration for all dependent upon her, or beneath her in station, endeared her memory to the people of England, even in spite of the party zeal and religious intolerance of the period in which she lived.

The authority from which the portrait was painted is a cotemporary miniature, half length, in the collection of the Duke of Buccleugh.

---

borough Cathedral to that in which Queen Katherine of Arragon was interred. Both monuments were destroyed by the soldiers of the Commonwealth.

Henry the Eighth.

ENRY VIII. was the second son of Henry VII. and Elizabeth of York. He was born on 28th of June, 1491. Although a prince, he was educated for the church, as, but for the death of his elder brother, Arthur, Prince of Wales, it was the intention of his father to place him at the head of the English church ; his training, therefore, qualified him to take that position as a controversialist in religion which formed a remarkable feature in his policy as a monarch. With a fine person, haughty manners, inheriting the great riches accumulated by his avaricious father, Henry indulged in all the extravagances and splendour of the period. His strong passions and warlike disposition ed him into great difficulties, alike domestic and political. With no conscientiousness, he made treaties and broke them, and marched armies into territories which he scarcely condescended to consider had any rights he had not authority o set aside. Henry VIII. may be considered the most absolute monarch who ever sat on the English throne, for he defied all alike,—church and nobles, foreign and domestic foes, and simply consulted his own will, whims, or passions, n all he did.

One of his first acts was to sacrifice the lives of two of his father's most devoted, though unprincipled, servants, Sir

Richard Empson and Edmund Dudley. This, however, was a popular measure with the people. He then married his brother Arthur's widow, Katherine of Arragon, in June, 1509; having ascended the throne on 22nd of April previous, when in his nineteenth year. After a war with France in the summer of 1513, in which he was triumphant, as also one with Scotland, carried on at the same time, against his own brother-in-law, James IV, which terminated in that king's death at Flodden Field, he commenced a course of reckless cruelty and rapacity, which terminated only in his own death many years afterwards. Bringing his polemical learning to bear upon the question of the Reformation, he attacked Luther and his doctrines in a work which gained for him the title of "Defender of the Faith" from the Pope. His utter want of anything like a true interest in religion is shown, however, in his subsequent conduct.

Falling in love with Anne Boleyn, he proceeded to divorce his queen, Katherine of Arragon, on the ground that, as she had been his brother's wife, she could not lawfully be his.

The beautiful and unfortunate Anne subsequently paid by her life for her sudden elevation, Henry declaring his daughter Mary, by Katherine of Arragon, and his daughter Elizabeth, by Anne Boleyn, both illegitimate. He then married Jane Seymour, who died a few days after giving birth to a son, afterwards Edward VI. His fourth wife was Anne of Cleves, whom he also divorced in order to marry Catherine Howard, niece of the Duke of Norfolk. In due course she was tried under attainder and executed; and he selected for his sixth wife Catherine Parr, who had already been married twice, both of her husbands being dead. His last queen, as also the divorced Anne of Cleves, survived him.

After confiscating the property of the church and dis-
tributing it in a most lavish and unwarrantable manner
amongst the nobles who helped him in his various schemes,
—warlike, political, and domestic, he finished his career on
28th of January, 1547, having that day signed an order for the
execution of his able and faithful general and minister, the
Duke of Norfolk, whose accomplished son, the Earl of
Surrey, he had nine days before consigned to the scaffold.

His only act of justice which can well be recorded, was
that of having dictated to one of his Parliaments the legal
recognition of his daughters, Mary and Elizabeth, as suc-
cessors to the throne in the event of his son Edward VI.
dying without issue.

The authorities from which the picture in the Prince's
Chamber was painted, are a fine Holbein in the Royal
Collection at Windsor Castle, and one at Hampton Court
Palace.

Anne Boleyn.

NNE BOLEYN, or Bullen, was the eldest daughter of Sir Thomas Bullen, afterwards Viscount Rochford, and Earl of Wiltshire and Ormond, and his wife Elizabeth Howard, daughter of Thomas second Duke of Norfolk, of that family. She was taken to France, when about seven years of age, by Mary, youngest sister of Henry VIII, when she married Louis XII, and remained with her until the death of that king, when she became one of the suite of Claude, queen of Francis I. Subsequently she lived with Margaret of Valois, Duchess of Alençon and Berri, afterwards queen of Henry IV. Some accounts, however, state that she returned to England with Queen Mary, and that soon after she became maid of honour to Katherine of Arragon. It was thus she was brought under the immediate notice of Henry VIII, who, in his passion for her, divorced his queen, the excellent Katherine.

Anne had been betrothed to Lord Percy, eldest son of the Duke of Northumberland; but although they were affectionately attached, the king, through the agency of Cardinal Wolsey, in whose household Lord Percy was, put an end to the engagement, and he was compelled to marry a daughter of the Earl of Shrewsbury. To conceal the king's part in this wicked act, Anne Boleyn was banished from the court for a time, but was soon brought back again, and created Marchioness of Pembroke in 1532.

The marriage ceremony between her and the king took place on 25th of January, 1533, and was performed by the then Bishop of Lichfield and Coventry, Rowland Lee :—a few of her relations, with the then newly-appointed Archbishop Cranmer, being present.

There is no doubt Cardinal Wolsey hated her for her attachment to the Protestant faith, which she had imbibed from Margaret of Valois. Her influence over the king was no doubt great, and Anne did not affect to be Wolsey's friend. Her first child, a son, died immediately after birth. This is said to have been a severe disappointment to the king. Subsequently she gave birth to a daughter, afterwards Queen Elizabeth.

Henry, in a fit of jealousy, arising probably out of some innocent indiscretion, as the queen is stated to have been of a lively, thoughtless disposition, given to gaiety and fond of display, caused her to be arrested on the river Thames as she returned from a tournament at Greenwich, on 1st of May, 1536. On 15th she was charged with high treason before the House of Peers, tried, and condemned.

Her execution was hastened by the king's new passion for Jane Seymour, and she was beheaded on Tower Hill, having protested her innocence of all the charges brought against her; and popular belief, if not historical proof, has long since cleared her memory of the imputations cast upon her.

The authority for the picture of Anne Boleyn, from which the photograph is taken, was painted from a small contemporary picture, half length—the painter of which is unknown—the property of Sir John P. Boileau, Bart.

Jane Seymour.

UEEN JANE SEYMOUR was the eldest daughter of Sir John Seymour, of Wolfe Hall, Wiltshire, a groom of the chamber to Henry VIII, and governor of Bristol Castle, and Margaret Wentworth, daughter of Sir Thomas Wentworth, of Nettlested, Suffolk.

She was maid of honour to Queen Anne Boleyn; and there is no doubt that her beauty attracting the attention of the king, and a sudden passion which he conceived for her, and which she encouraged, hastened, if it did not absolutely cause, the downfall of her unfortunate mistress. So little did Henry care for law, decency, or public opinion, that on the day after Anne Boleyn's execution he profaned the rite of marriage by having it performed between himself and Jane Seymour. This took place on 20th of May, 1536, at Wolfe Hall, Wiltshire, and on 8th of June Parliament created a law to settle the Crown on the issue of this so-called marriage, to the exclusion of the Princesses Mary and Elizabeth, the former being the daughter of Queen Katherine, and the latter of Queen Anne Boleyn.

The character of this, the third wife of Henry VIII. can scarcely be said to have had time to develope itself, for fifteen months after her union with the king she died, at Hampton Court, two days after giving birth to a son, afterwards the amiable and excellent King Edward VI. This is gene-

rally supposed to have occurred on 14th of October, 1537, the prince having been born on 12th of that month.

The joy of the king, and the people too, at the birth of a prince is said to have been very great; and the depression and sorrow which ensued upon the death of the queen was no doubt in proportion.

Her death was chiefly to be attributed to the absurd custom then prevalent, by which the queen was compelled to keep her chamber for one month prior to accouchement, and the still more reprehensible etiquette which necessitated, in Queen Jane Seymour's case, her presence, on the third day after the birth of the heir to the throne, at the public baptism of her son. She was buried with great pomp at Windsor, and, strange to say, the disinherited Princess Mary was the official chief mourner.

The authorities for the portrait are a copy by Remée, of a picture by Holbein, destroyed by fire at Whitehall, a small Holbein in the collection of the Society of Antiquaries, and a picture in the collection of the Marquis of Aylesbury.

Anne of Cleves.

ENRY VIII. had been a widower nearly three years after the death of Queen Jane Seymour when he married his fourth wife, Anne, second daughter of John, Duke of Cleves, and Marie, heiress of William, Duke of Juliers, Berg, and Ravensburgh. She was born on 22nd of September, 1516, and was educated in the Protestant faith, as her father had adopted the Lutheran doctrines. Sybella of Cleves, her elder sister, was the wife of John Frederick of Saxony, so famous as the "Lion-hearted Elector," and as the great champion of the Reformation. This princess was celebrated for her virtues, talents, beauty, and amiable manners; but, above all, for her indomitable energy and perseverance. In this she was a strange contrast to her sister Anne, who was of a very quiet and passive disposition.

It was chiefly through the agency of Cromwell that the daughters of the Duke of Cleves were brought under the notice of King Henry VIII, and as the elder sister's character and attainments had become known, it was hoped that either Anne or the youngest daughter, Amelie, would be acceptable to the king. Accordingly, Hans Holbein, the celebrated painter to Henry's court, was commissioned to paint portraits of both. The king's choice fell upon Anne, to whom he had been predisposed by the favourable accounts sent by the agents of Cromwell.

The chivalrous Elector, John Frederick, opposed the match, as he objected to the character of Henry as a husband ; but his objections were overruled on the ground that the cause of the Reformation might be promoted by a Protestant queen of England. After a delay, in consequence of the death of Anne's father, the preparations for the marriage were completed on 6th of February, 1539 ; Cromwell being especially anxious for the union, as a triumph over Gardiner, Norfolk, and others of the Privy Council attached to the cause of the church of Rome. Henry never forgave him for his activity in this matter, since the accounts sent by his agents so raised the king's expectations as to the beauty of his new bride, that, when these expectations were not realized, the disappointment was not regulated by facts, but was in proportion to his own revulsion of feeling. For Anne of Cleves was no more the ugly and uninteresting person the king wished to make out she was, after their first interview, than the paragon of beauty and grace which Cromwell and his agents had depicted her. Holbein's portrait, too, was probably true enough as a picture, except in one particular, which artists rarely, if ever, attempt to depict, for Anne was marked with the small-pox, the effects of which the picture did not show ; and the regularity of her features and her complexion, as shown in the painting, suffered a great drawback when seen in the reality. Holbein was so little given to· flattery that, but for this fact, it would be difficult to account for the wrong impression conveyed to Henry's mind by a picture from his hand.

The marriage contract was signed at Dusseldorf on 4th of September, 1539, and Anne arrived at Calais, on her way to England, on 11th of December, where she was received by the officers of the English king ; and it is recorded that, out of the six queens of Henry VIII, there were relatives of five of them in the company. She landed at Dover on 27th of December, and arrived at Rochester on New Year's-eve, and spent New Year's-day, 1540, at the Bishop's palace. Here her first meeting with Henry took place, and the king's dream of her beauty was dissolved, probably as much by her tasteless and uncouth dress as anything else. The chroniclers vary in their accounts of the king's estimate of his bride, but all agree as to his disappointment; and Lord Russell stated "that he never saw his highness so marvellously astonished and abashed as on that occasion,"—meaning at the first interview.

Anne was probably not much more impressed, since the king was no longer young; but she received him very humbly and meekly, which soothed him in some degree. His evil disposition was, however, not to be conciliated, and he sought to find reasons for the non-completion of his engagement; but failed in doing so.

The marriage was solemnized on 6th of January, 1540, at Greenwich, in the midst of much pomp and ceremony. For some weeks after the marriage the king treated his newly-made queen with respect, and at least a show of affection. Her ignorance of the English language, and especially of music, of which Henry was very fond, together with her want of learning, were all against her, otherwise, by all accounts, she was a comely young woman of four-and-twenty, the king being twice that age, and far from attractive in appearance. Four or five months were, however, quite sufficient to decide Henry to dissolve his marriage with Anne of Cleves, in spite of all her attempts to conciliate him. At length, taking advantage of some negotiations which had been opened for a contract between herself and Francis of Lorraine, prior to her engagement to Henry, of which she reminded him by saying, "If she had not been

compelled to marry him, she might have fulfilled her engagement with another," Henry found his tender conscience
once more a matter of difficulty, as in the case of Queen
Katherine; but on this occasion it was compunction for
having married a Protestant.

In due course all the machinery of intrigue, threats, and
violation of law, were set to work, and in the end the
marriage was declared " null and void." When Anne was
waited upon by the commissioners of the king, to inform
her of the decision, she fainted, because she fancied they
were about to convey her to the Tower; but on learning that
she was to have estates worth £3000 a-year, and take
precedence of all ladies except the king's daughters, she
resigned all her honours as queen very quickly, and with so
much indifference, that Henry was rather piqued than otherwise, as it tended to lower him in his own estimation.
Henceforth, Anne of Cleves, Gulech, Gildee, and Berg,
became the loving sister of Henry Tudor, and decided to
spend the remainder of her life in England.

While residing at Richmond, the king visited her there,
on 6th of August, after the divorce was pronounced. She
received him graciously, and such was his glee and good
temper, that some people thought he was about to pay his
addresses to her again..

Anne's family treated the matter with a lofty scorn, and
her brother, the Duke of Cleves, sarcastically told the
Bishop of Bath, that " he was glad his sister had fared no
worse."

In less than a year and a-half after her own repudiation,
Anne of Cleves received the intelligence of the fate of her
successor, Catherine Howard.

Anne kept up a friendly intercourse with the king's
children. The Princess Mary visited her in June, 1543.

On 26th of June, 1550, she visited the court of King Edward VI, and the young monarch interested himself to obtain a grant of money for her from the Parliament, as she had fallen in debt. She acquired the English language so far as to write it with fluency, and she corresponded with the king's children pretty regularly. She attended the coronation of Queen Mary, riding in the same carriage with the Princess Elizabeth, afterwards queen. This was her last public appearance. Her last place of residence was at Dartford, Kent, at one of the abbeys suppressed by Henry VIII, which he had used as a hunting-seat. She died, however, at the Palace of Chelsea, on 16th of July, 1557, and was buried on 3rd of August in Westminster Abbey, with much magnificence. Her tomb is near the high altar, in a place of special honour, at the feet of King Sebert, the founder of the Abbey.

Anne of Cleves was humble and unambitious in a remarkable degree. Her life, after the divorce from the king, was a placid and happy one except for pecuniary difficulties. Her beneficence was great, and though brought up a Lutheran, it is clear, from her will, that she died a member of the Church of Rome.

The authorities for this portrait are an etching by Hollar, half length, apparently from a miniature in the possession of Colonel Meyrick, which is very probably the miniature painted by Holbein for Henry VIII ; this miniature, and one in the possession of his grace the Duke of Buccleuch.

Catherine Howard.

ATHERINE HOWARD, the fifth queen of King Henry VIII, was the second daughter and fifth child of Lord Edmund Howard, ninth son of the Earl of Surrey, the victor at Flodden Field, and Joyce, widow of Sir John Leigh, Knight, a daughter of Sir Richard Culpepper, of Hollingbourne, Kent. She was born in 1521 or 1522, probably at Lambeth, as the Howards had a residence there, at which the brother of Lord Edmund, the Duke of Norfolk, resided when attending the court of Henry; and it was here, too, that the Dowager Duchess, step-mother of the Duke, kept great state.

Few men contributed more to the victory at Flodden than the father of Catherine Howard, for he was Marshal of the English under his able father, Surrey. With a younger son's portion, he married for affection, and had to struggle through the depths of poverty, and still to remember that he was a nobleman; but through the interest of his cousin, Anne Boleyn, when she was all-powerful with the king, Lord Edmund obtained the post of comptroller at Calais. Prior to this, his wife, the mother of Catherine, had died comparatively young, sinking, it is supposed, under the privations to which she and her brave husband had been subjected; several of her children being still very young.

Catherine was brought up, during her early years, by her

mother's brother, Sir John Culpepper, at Hollingbourne, as the playmate of his son and heir, Thomas Culpepper, who was subsequently mixed up with the charges made against her when she was queen. After her father's second marriage she was taken into the great establishment of Agnes, Dowager Duchess of Norfolk, who shamefully neglected her.

There are few positions in human life more perilous or more pitiable than that of a young motherless girl confided to the care of relatives, who, taking little personal interest in her welfare, allow her to associate with dependents and servants; yet such was the early fate of Catherine Howard. Giving early promise of much personal beauty and of a lively disposition, she first attracted the attention of a player on the virginals, attached to the suite of the duchess, and who was her instructor in music. Subsequently another clandestine courtship sprang up, promoted no doubt by the intrigues of the waiting-women of the duchess. Amongst the gentlemen of the household troop of the Duke of Norfolk was Francis Derham, a distant relative of the Howards, who became greatly attached to Catherine, and he proposed to make her his wife; and, no doubt, under the persuasion of the women amongst whom she was thrown, Catherine entered into something very like a betrothal, and being fond of finery, natural enough to one so young, she accepted money and presents of dresses and jewellery from Derham. The whole matter was kept secret from the dowager duchess, and much duplicity was shown on the part of Derham, and probably also of Catherine, to account for the possession of the coveted silks and satins; which the former supplied, under the understanding that she was to pay him for them at a future time.

All this went on until it is proved that a plighting of

troth took place between them; and as this act was then binding in the eye of the church, and consequently of the law, it often happened that it was an impediment to subsequent marriage with any other person. The character of the contract between Catherine Howard and Francis Derham may be judged of by the fact that "Derham asked her permission to call her 'wife' and entreated her to call him 'husband,' to which Catherine replied 'she was content that it should be so.'"*

The corrupting influences by which the future Queen of England was surrounded at this time is acknowledged on all hands, and the dowager duchess did not interfere until it was too late, when she beat both Catherine and Derham, and boxed the ears of Mistress Bulmer, one of her waiting-women, for permitting romping and presumptuous levity, on Derham's part, with her young kinswoman; but she did not dismiss Derham, as she probably regarded the whole matter as a passing indiscretion. Subsequently the duchess discovered the real position in which the page stood to her young kinswoman, and again Catherine suffered, after a rude fashion, from blows. Derham had to fly to Ireland, and it must have been at this time that Catherine uttered the words recorded against her, it is said with tears streaming down her cheeks, "Thou wilt never live to say to me 'thou hast swerved.'"

After this the dowager duchess cleared her household of the waiting-women who had so abused her confidence. One, however, appears to have remained, who acted as letter writter between Catherine and Derham. The latter returned from Ireland in due time, and interfered between Catherine and her cousin, Thomas Culpepper, to whom it

---

* Miss Strickland's "Queens of England."

D

was reported she was about to be married. He also interfered to prevent her going to the court of Anne of Cleves,
to which her cousin, who is described as " a most beautiful
youth," was attached as a page. In the end Derham had
again to disappear, as Catherine treated him with coldness
and disdain; probably from estimating his real character and
her own indiscretion.

At this period Catherine Howard was considered a young
gentlewoman of great natural reserve, much grace, and of
modest maidenly deportment.

King Henry VIII. first saw his last victim at a banquet
given on the occasion of his marriage with Anne of Cleves.
He was struck with her wit and grace. Gardiner saw the
advantage which might arise from the selection of Catherine,
a member of the Church of Rome, to succeed or displace
Anne of Cleves, a Protestant, and took care that the king
should not lack opportunities for meeting his new flame.
So Catherine was appointed maid of honour to Anne of
Cleves, just as her cousin-german Anne Boleyn had been to
Katherine of Arragon; but her conduct was very different
to that of her relative or Jane Seymour, for she treated her
mistress with great respect and consideration.

The dowager duchess no sooner saw that her young and
formerly despised relative was to be the future Queen of
England, than she paid her every attention, furnished her
with suitable clothes, jewels, and such array as became a
daughter of the house of Howard. Knowing the past, and
fearful of Derham, she was anxious to know where he was,
and not being satisfied with what she could learn from her
retainers, she imprudently revived the thoughts of the past
by asking Catherine herself, when the latter is said to have
replied, that " she did not know where he was become."

Of course there were others to fear besides Derham, and

Mistress Jane Bulmer reminded Catherine of her existence and hopes, by writing her a letter in which she states her hope that " the Queen of Britain will not forget her secretary."

Henry's marriage with his fifth queen was solemnized very quickly after the dissolution of his union with Anne of Cleves. There is no record of the ceremony, but Catherine Howard was present at the chapel at Hampton Court Palace, on 8th of August, 1540, seated by the side of the king, and afterwards dined in public. Her youngest step-daughter, the child of her cousin Anne Boleyn, was placed opposite to her at the table, and she always gave the princess, as her relative, the place of honour after herself, during her short career of royalty.

The congratulations on this so-called auspicious union appear to have been general. The family connections of Catherine and her relationship to the king's second wife were considered as rendering the marriage quite appropriate.

Henry took his new bride from place to place during the autumn of 1540, and in October the court returned to Windsor, where Christmas was spent. The spring and early summer of 1541 were spent at Greenwich, Eltham, and in a progress through Kent, Essex, and some of the midland counties.

At length whispers began to be heard against the new queen. The struggle between the Romish and Protestant parties still continued. Catherine's relative, the Duke of Norfolk, and Gardiner, Bishop of Winchester, were of the former faction, whilst Archbishop Cranmer was as decidedly of the latter. The Roman Catholics had failed to get up an insurrection in Yorkshire, and the king, accompanied by his new queen, visited this county to receive the submission of the delinquent party. Vengeance on the part of the king, tempered by mercy through the influence of the queen, was the order of the day; and the rebellious citizens offered the king sums of money as a propitiation, instead of the lives of the prisoners taken in the late revolt.

It was during this progress that Queen Catherine Howard imprudently consented, possibly with great reluctance, to receive her former betrothed husband, Francis Derham, as a gentleman in waiting at her court. The date of the appointment is given as that of 27th of August, 1541. It is said that he acted as her secretary on several occasions, and as there is no evidence that she could write, possibly her correspondence with such people as Mistress Jane Bulmer required Derham, or some other person equally versed in the affairs of her youth, to write her letters. At this time, too, the queen's cousin, Thomas Culpepper, had fallen into sad disgrace, and had just been pardoned by the king for a crime aggravated by murder in resisting apprehension. Catherine imprudently, but no doubt from kindly motives, granted him a private interview, and it is said gave him some of her jewels to relieve his pecuniary necessities. Her confident in this matter was a wicked and unscrupulous woman, Lady Rochford, the wife of Anne Boleyn's brother, who had assisted in the destruction of her own husband, and her unfortunate sister-in-law.

At length the early life of Catherine became known to Cranmer, and under such circumstances that he felt compelled, after consulting with the Lord Chancellor, and the Earl of Hertford, to bring the matter before the king. Besides, the opportunity for a blow at Gardiner and the Duke of Norfolk, as the leaders of the Romish party, was too tempting to be resisted.

Henry, who appears to have been devotedly attached to his young wife, for she had borne herself so modestly and with much grace, was astounded at the charges, and at first refused to believe them; but as conviction was forced upon him, it is stated that he shed tears. On the very day before the information reached him, he had ordered a form of public thanksgiving to be prepared by the Bishop of Lincoln, that it had pleased God to bless him with "so loving, dutiful, and virtuous a queen."

Derham, Culpepper, and others, were arrested; the matter was fully investigated, and Henry's jealousy once roused, the usual result followed. Derham and Culpepper, after being questioned by torture, from which nothing new resulted, were executed at Tyburn on 9th of December, 1541, the former being hung, and the latter beheaded. The Dowager Duchess of Norfolk and Lady Rochford, with others, were also arrested; and no time was lost in passing a bill of attainder through both houses of Parliament. This was read a first time on 21st of January, 1542, and finally passed on 6th of February. On 10th of February, Catherine was removed to the Tower of London; but not without difficulty. The royal assent was given to the bill on 11th, and on 13th she was beheaded, with Lady Rochford.

Catherine Howard submitted to her fate with courage and humility, and probably more sympathy would have been felt for her had she died with a less infamous person than the woman who helped so materially to destroy Anne Boleyn, by an accusation against her own husband, the brother of the latter queen.

The aged Duchess of Norfolk was subsequently released after a long period of confinement.

The body of Catherine Howard was carried from the scaffold, and interred in a grave by the side of that of Anne Boleyn, in St. Peter's chapel, in the Tower. Subsequently, in the reign of Mary, the attainder under which she was executed, was annulled, as it never received Henry's signature, and therefore it was not valid.   Thus Catherine Howard was in reality murdered.

The authority for the portrait is a miniature of the period in the collection of the Duke of Buccleuch.

Katherine Parr.

HE sixth wife of Henry VIII. was Katherine Parr, daughter of Sir Thomas Parr, of Kendal, Westmoreland, and Maud, daughter and co-heiress of Sir Thomas Greene, of Greene's Norton, Northamptonshire. She was said to have been born in 1510; but there is evidence, in a letter written by her mother, that she was not born until 1513, at Kendal Castle. She first married, at an early age, Edward Borough, eldest son of Thomas, Lord Borough of Gainsborough, a gentleman of middle age, with a family; who, dying shortly after their union, left her a widow in her fifteenth or sixteenth year. She then married John Neville, Lord Latimer, probably before she was twenty. He also had a family, and though no children were born to her of either marriage, she had the satisfaction of attending to the education of the children of both her husbands; and the discipline thus gained, alike in learning as in worldly management, no doubt had a remarkable effect upon her character, and she was highly esteemed by all who had the privilege of knowing her. The death of Lord Latimer left her again a widow, about 1543, with a reputation for much integrity and worth. Still young, rich, and highly accomplished, she became attached to Sir Thomas Seymour, the brother of Queen Jane Seymour. He was considered the handsomest man at the court of King Henry VIII, and was distinguished

for his gaiety and the magnificence of his dress, which all
tried to follow. That Lady Latimer, so learned, grave, and
devout, should fix her affections on such a man seems unac-
countable, but it is pretty certain that her reluctance to
marry the king, and some sharp and cutting rebuffs she
administered to him when his addresses first became clear
to her, arose out of her desire to marry Seymour. The
latter, however, did not care to enter the lists against such
a rival as Henry, whose easy method of disposing of those
who stood in his way was proverbial, and so he left the
Court with the best grace he could, and Lady Latimer
became Queen of England with the usual rapidity with
which King Henry effected his matrimonial engagements.

There was none of the secresy about the marriage of
Katherine Parr which had characterized Henry's unions
with his other subjects, especially Anne Boleyn and Catherine Howard, and the ceremony took place at Hampton
Court Palace on 12th of July, 1543, a few months after the
death of Lord Latimer. She must have then been thirty
years of age, and not thirty-three, or thirty four, as stated
by some authorities. King Henry was fifty-two.

Her talents were no doubt considerable. She had received
an excellent education, had great experience of life, especially in the domestic circle, and was, therefore, well quali-
fied to act as the companion to a king whose abilities were
certainly above the average of the men of his time, and
whose age led him to less frivolous pursuits than those
which had characterized his youth.

Possessing great affability, dignity, and simplicity of
manners, Katherine Parr seems to have filled her station
rather like an English matron than a queen. For the third
time a step-mother, she again exercised her influence for
the benefit and happiness of her husband's children, and the

king's daughters, Mary and Elizabeth, were restored to their proper positions at Court; and the privy purse of both was often replenished by their kindly-natured and wealthy step-mother.

Embracing the reformed religion, after careful consideration, and from a strong conviction of its Scriptural truth, Katherine appears not to have left the Church of Rome until after the death of Lord Latimer. Favourably known to the king before she became a widow the second time, it is said that even then she possessed a great influence over him; no doubt from her ability to support her own position by her learning and ready wit, but also by the more legitimate power of a virtuous and consistent life.

The only difficulty which ever appears to have arisen between the king and herself was on the matter of his famous six articles, of which he had enjoined the observance as a means of conciliating the Church of Rome; and the prohibition of the printing and circulation of English versions of the New Testament. The queen, as a zealous Protestant, argued with the king on these points, her singular courage causing her to forget that she was no longer Lady Latimer. As a matter of course this raised her up many enemies, amongst others Gardiner, Bishop of Winchester, and Wriothesly, Lord Chancellor, and she nearly fell a victim to a plot to impeach her and the ladies of her court, several of whom were her relatives. A copy of the articles of accusation to be made against her accidentally fell into her hands. With great tact and judgment she so conducted herself to Henry during a visit he paid whilst she was ill, in consequence of anxiety of mind arising out of this discovery, that he was convinced that she had not intended to influence his judgment in relation to matters of State or the Church. The conspirators were overwhelmed with reproaches by the king himself, whose renewed confidence was shown by his appointing her Regent during his expedition to France in 1544. In his will he mentions " her great love, obedience, chasteness of life, and wisdom;" but Katherine appears to have been disappointed that he did not leave her Regent during the minority of Edward VI.

After three years and six months of royalty, Katherine retired on the death of the king, on 28th of January, 1546-7, to her jointure palace at Chelsea, and here her former lover, Sir Thomas, now Lord Seymour of Sudeley, Lord High Admiral of England, quickly renewed his suit, and was favourably received. They were privately married in May, within four months after King Henry's death. Strangely enough the young King Edward VI. was induced to believe that he had recommended his uncle Seymour to his step-mother as a husband.

Katherine Parr's fourth marriage was as unhappy as her previous unions had been prosperous. Seymour treated her with great harshness, and it is supposed had a scheme for marrying the Princess Elizabeth, afterwards queen, who had been confided to the care of Katherine.

Although she had no children by her previous marriages, this unhappy union with Seymour gave her hopes of a family; but she died in child-bed, at Sudeley Castle, Gloucestershire, a seat of Lord Seymour's, on 5th of September, 1548, and was buried in the chapel there.

Katherine Parr was learned, and fond of literature, and the more refined pursuits of the women of her age. She united the dignity of learning with the earnestness of the Christian, and was pious without bigotry or intolerance of the opinions of others. This is shown by the intercourse which existed between herself and her step-daughter the princess, afterwards Queen Mary, notwithstanding the great difference in their religious opinions. In 1545 she published a volume of collected prayers and meditations, with fifteen psalms, and other devotional pieces of her own composition. She also wrote a work, printed after her death, " The Lamentation of a Sinner bewailing the ignorance of a blind Life." In these compositions are passages of as great beauty as any in the English language.

Katherine's daughter, Mary, her only child, was left, after the execution of Lord Seymour in 1549, to the care of her mother's friend, the Duchess of Suffolk, who appears to have meanly complained of the trust. Her uncles, both the Protector Somerset (Seymour's brother), and the Marquis of Northampton, withheld the property to which she was heiress in the right of both father and mother; and though some accounts state that she died in her infancy, it appears that she lived to become the wife of Sir Edward Bushel.

Katherine Parr was of short stature, *petite* and beautiful in form and feature.

The authority for this portrait is a life-size picture of the period in the possession of the Earl of Denbigh.

Edward the Sixth.

KING EDWARD VI, whose memory is commemorated by so many noble schools of learning bearing his name in our day, was the son of Henry VIII. and his queen, Jane Seymour. He was born at Hampton Court Palace on 12th of October, 1537, he died in his sixteenth year, at Greenwich, on 6th of July, 1553.

Succeeding to the throne before he was ten years old, he was placed under the guardianship of Seymour, Duke of Somerset, his mother's brother, as Lord Protector. Between this nobleman and Dudley, Duke of Northumberland, a terrible struggle ensued for the possession of both the king's person and authority, which ended in the accusation of Seymour of high treason, of which he was found guilty, and for which he was beheaded. From that event, until the death of King Edward, Northumberland was the guardian, and he so used his power and influence with the young and amiable monarch, that he brought ruin upon himself and his estimable daughter-in-law, Lady Jane Grey, by inducing Edward to settle the succession of the crown upon her.

The attainments of King Edward VI. are very remarkable. In spite of the difficulties of his position, placed as he was between two opposing factions, with little or no authority, and of a delicate constitution, his love of knowledge and great natural abilities enabled him to master several

languages. He spoke French, Spanish, and Italian, and is said to have had a critical knowledge of Latin and Greek. He was well acquainted with astronomy, logic, and the philosophy of his time, and gained a good theoretical knowledge of military arts, especially that of fortification. The ability with which he examined into the conduct of public men, and the acuteness with which he detected peculiarities of character, and sought to correct mal-administration, give evidence of great undeveloped powers. The famous Cardan said of him, " This child was so bred, had such parts, was of such expectation, that he looked like a miracle of a man ; and in him was such an attempt of Nature, that not only England, but the world, had reason to lament his being so early snatched away."

His great abilities did not make him proud or conceited. He was particularly gracious and kind in his manner to all persons, patient, good-natured, affable, and sincere. When public occasions required it, he assumed the majesty of the king and grave demeanour of the statesman ; but was always the gentleman and scholar. He enjoyed himself with simplicity and dignity in a way suited to his age and rank ; had great courage, and, whilst he was bountiful without extravagance, he was religious without intolerance.

No better evidence of his great ability, as also of the excellence of his character, can be given than the journal which he kept from the commencement of his reign until nearly its close, and now preserved in the Cotton Library, British Museum. This proves, in his own hand, that the eulogies bestowed upon him were not the inventions of partial friends or flattering courtiers. In this journal the events of his daily life are recorded with great simplicity and truthfulness, and show his love of knowledge, his appreciation of the political events of his time, and his interest in the domestic comfort, and good municipal government of his people.

The difficulties of Edward's position in the early years of his reign, standing as he did between two such men as his uncle Seymour, as Protector, and Dudley, as the leader of the nobility against the authority of his relative, must have had a serious effect upon a naturally delicate constitution. In a letter written by him in the latter part of 1547, when he was scarcely ten years old, the painfulness of his position, as well as his premature sagacity, is shown in a very interesting form.

His personal appearance is described as having been very pleasing. Sir John Heywood says, " He was of body beautiful; of sweet aspect, and especially in his eyes, which seemed to have a starry loveliness and lustre in them.''

His weakness of body, however, increased,—consumption finally set in; and, as already stated, he died in his sixteenth year, to the great regret of his people, whose interests there can be no doubt he had deeply at heart.

The authority for the portrait is a very fine Holbein, three-quarter length, in the Royal Collection at Windsor Castle.

Queen Mary.

QUEEN MARY was the eldest daughter of King Henry VIII. and his first queen, Katherine of Arragon. She was born at the palace of Greenwich, on 8th of February, 1516.

There can be little doubt that a disposition by no means naturally amiable, was much warped and rendered hard and unbending by the early treatment she received at the hands of her father. Without possessing any striking qualities either for good or evil, the position in which she was placed from childhood was not calculated to promote either her happiness or the development of any special characteristic ; but, on the contrary, to induce her to conceal as much as possible her own feelings in relation to those around her.

The religious views in which she had been educated, and to which she clung with the tenacity of a nature rendered suspicious by ill-usage, but in which she no doubt found many consolations from her isolation from public affairs, rendered her an object of suspicion to a government and a people whose growing tendencies were more and more towards the new-born Reformation.

Her marriage, too, with Philip of Spain was very unpopular with a large section of the English people, and tended to embitter the feelings which had sprung up in their minds against her ; whilst the cruel neglect with which her hus-

Philip the Second of Spain.

HE Archduke Philip of Spain, the only son of the Emperor Charles V. and Isabella of Portugal, was born on 21st of May, 1527. His father having abdicated the Spanish throne in January, 1556, Philip became king, not only of Spain, but of the Two Sicilies, Milan, and other Italian provinces, as also of the possessions in the newly-settled continent of America; and the phrase which has been applied in modern times to the British empire was true of the extent of that of Spain, under Philip,—"that the sun never set upon his dominions."

Philip was married four times. His first wife was his cousin Mary of Portugal: the unfortunate Don Carlos was the only offspring of this union. His second wife was Mary, Queen of England, eldest daughter of King Henry VIII, to whom he acted as a cold, cruel, and heartless husband, and by whom, happily, he had no children. His third wife was the Princess Elizabeth of France, who, strange to say, had been originally betrothed to Don Carlos, thus giving rise to much romantic speculation as to the cause of the abiding enmity which existed between the father and son, resulting in the death of the latter in his twenty-third year. His fourth wife was Anne, daughter of the Emperor Maximilian II, and the mother of Philip's only son and successor. Two daughters were also born of his marriage with Elizabeth of France.

Philip's personal character was productive of many evils to Europe. His vast possessions, and the political power left in his hands by his father Charles V, were terrible weapons for one so naturally stern, proud, and morose. Educated by his fanatical parent in the strictest formulas of the Church of Rome, and with a nation on which such teachings could not fail to have the worst possible effect, Philip of Spain was a scourge to his own subjects alike in Spain, Italy, and the Netherlands, and a standing menace to France and England, in consequence of the progress which the new principles of the Reformation were making in both countries. With a savage sincerity which completely absolves him from the charge of hypocrisy, or of using, as his father had done, his religious opinions as a means to political power, Philip persecuted his subjects at home in person, and in Holland by emissaries, such as the notorious and ferocious Duke of Alva; whilst in Italy and Naples fire and sword did their work upon all suspected of heresy. Aiming at reducing France and England to subjection in the interests of the Church of Rome, he united with Catherine de Medici in the destruction of the Huguenots in the former, whilst in 1588 he dispatched to the shores of the latter his so-called "Invincible Armada," by which he hoped to terrify or subdue Queen Elizabeth and the English people.

His reign closed in bitterness, and with a full consciousness of failure. His intolerance and ambition were completely frustrated. His contest with the Netherlands, during which Alva alone is said to have boasted that in less than six years he had destroyed 18,000 heretics at the stake, ended in his having to abdicate his right to reign over the whole of the provinces of the Low Countries, in favour of his daughter Isabella and her husband the Archduke Albert, as the only means of retaining the sovereignty in his family.

The haughty spirit must indeed have been broken which could submit to such a measure. Nor were his mental conflicts and penalties the only ones which he had to bear. Suffering from prolonged and fearful maladies, he died in 1598, at the age of seventy-two years ; the same year in which he was compelled to conclude the treaty of Vervins with King Henry IV. of France, which gave peace to Western Europe.

The authority for the portrait is a fine picture, half length, said to be by Titian, in the collection of Earl Stanhope.

Queen Elizabeth.

QUEEN ELIZABETH was the second and only surviving child of Henry VIII. and Anne Boleyn. She was born at the palace at Greenwich on 7th of September, 1533. That she had considerable natural ability is certain; and although the extravagant praises of her wisdom as a monarch are now received with caution, yet her shrewdness and common-sense choice of the ministers who made her reign famous, must always be regarded as no mean evidence of mental power. Educated as the repudiated daughter of the king, in common with her paternal sister Mary, her position was a very equivocal one. Nor did the fact that Parliament, at the instigation of the king, replaced her and Mary as entitled to their proper succession to the throne, conduce to her happiness and comfort; since it led to the two sisters regarding each other with jealousy, the more especially that they differed in their religious opinions, and became thus to be considered as the representatives of the two parties into which the kingdom was divided—Mary as representing the interests of the Church of Rome, and Elizabeth those of the Reformed Church.

At the death of Henry VIII, Elizabeth was placed under the guardianship of his widow Queen Katherine Parr. The sudden marriage of the latter with the Lord Admiral Seymour, brother of the Duke of Somerset, Protector to the young

King Edward VI, threw Elizabeth very much into the power of this nobleman; and evidence is in existence that he had hoped to have brought about a marriage with her; but the intention being discovered by the ministers of Edward, the princess was taken from his charge.

After this she was thrown more into the society of her admirable brother, the youthful king; and as she was fond of learning, acquired languages readily, as well as sympathized with him in his attachment to the Reformed Faith, it is possible that this was one of the happiest periods of the life of Elizabeth, as they pursued their studies together, whilst the amiable character of the young monarch could not fail to be a source of comfort to his sister.

After the death of Edward VI, Elizabeth espoused the cause of Mary against that of Lady Jane Grey; but although received with favour at Court, she was still an object of jealousy in many ways, and during Mary's reign she suffered many indignities. At her sister's death, on 17th of November, 1558, Elizabeth, then in her twenty-sixth year, ascended the throne, and the people evinced their hopes in her by the most extravagant rejoicings. Fortunately for Elizabeth and the nation, she had chosen a honest and capable minister in Cecil, Lord Burleigh; but for this, her attachment to such a man as Robert Dudley, whom she created Earl of Leicester, would have been fatal to her government; for he ambitiously aspired to her hand, and would have probably succeeded but for the influence which Cecil had with the queen.

Elizabeth never married, although she appears to have amused her Council, Parliament, and people with many negotiations, which appeared to lead them to hope that she would select a consort, as in their anxiety respecting the succession to the crown, they were anxious she should do. It is doubtful if ever she seriously contemplated marriage, as her love of power and intense vanity were clearly against the possibility of finding any one equal to the high position of her husband.

The political events of Elizabeth's reign were of the greatest importance to the future progress of popular power in England. Her intrigues in support of the reforming party in Scotland involved an amount of encouragement in the same direction in England, which nothing in subsequent reigns could check. Excommunicated by Pope Pius V. in 1571,—attacked by Spain at a later period,—and surrounded by foreign foes, all served to throw her more and more upon her people ; and out of the weakness of the monarch the strength of the nation grew.

Elizabeth's unscrupulous conduct in many things, especially in her imprisonment of Mary Queen of Scots for a period of nineteen years, and the final execution of that misguided, but unfortunate monarch, are blots upon her character and reign, which no admiration for her indomitable courage can efface. Her envy, dislike, and final hatred of Mary Stuart was something to be wondered at, and certainly not to be accounted for by the difference in religious views. Violent, headstrong, given to strange fits of blustering passion, and a weakness in some things unworthy of the meanest of her subjects, she possessed also many of the qualities which were essential to the times in which she lived ; and thus her reign has been regarded as, on the whole, a successful and even brilliant one for England and the English.

Her death was hastened, if not absolutely occasioned, by grief and remorse for the execution of her last favourite, the Earl of Essex, whom she survived only two years. She died in her seventieth year, on 24th of March, 1603.

The portrait is executed from a small whole length picture by Lucas de Heere, at Hampton Court.

Louis the Twelfth of France.

OUIS XII. of France, popularly called "Le Père du Peuple," commenced his reign in 1498, having succeeded his cousin Charles VIII. Being still a youth when his father, the Duke of Orleans, brother of Louis XI, died, he was placed under the guardianship of that strange mixture of cunning, cruelty, and superstition, and suffered much indignity. At a later period he was exiled and imprisoned in consequence of his disputes with the mother of Charles VIII, Anne lady of Beaujeu, afterwards Duchess of Bourbon. These trials taught him many things which were useful and beneficial to him when he became king; and the title of "Father of the People" seems to have been well earned, considering the period at which he lived ; for no king of France had ever been more desirous to promote the well-being and happiness of his people.

His unfortunate propensity, however, to war, was frequently very ruinous from being entered into without foresight; thus bringing misery upon his country, when a more peaceable policy would have produced comfort and prosperity.

Louis had been married, very much against his inclination, and at an early age, to Joan, the youngest daughter of Louis XI. On becoming king he sued for a divorce, and obtained it from the wicked and cruel Pope Alexander VI, whose

son, Cæsar Borgia, he created Duke of Valentinois. He then married Anne of Bretagne, the widow of the late King Charles VIII, on 18th of January, 1499, who died in January, 1514.

The wars, intrigues, and political changes of the period ultimately wearied the king;—one of his most formidable enemies being Henry VIII. of England, then young and full of ambitious projects. After the death of his queen, whom he loved with sincere affection, although often angry with her for interfering in political affairs, he concluded a peace with Henry, and negotiated for the hand of the young and beautiful Princess Mary, sister of the English king, who, although already privately engaged, it is said, to the Duke of Suffolk, was taken to France in the latter part of 1514, and became his wife; a victim to state policy. A prior public contract with Charles of Spain being set aside to meet the wishes of her imperious brother, Henry.

Louis did not survive his third marriage many months. He was anxious to promote the comfort and happiness of his young bride, and gave up his former quiet way of living, and entered into the fashionable gaieties of the time. He dined at twelve at noon instead of at eight in the morning, as formerly, and remained taking part in gay meetings until midnight, instead of retiring at six, as had previously been his custom. This change produced ill health, and he died on 1st of January, 1515.

The authorities employed in the execution of the portrait are a fine highly-finished missal picture, the property of the Right Hon. H. Labouchere, M.P., and a figure in the collection of Count Veil-Castel.

Princess Mary.

THIS princess was the second surviving daughter of Henry VII. and his queen, Elizabeth Woodville, and sister to King Henry VIII. She was born in 1498.

While still a child a contract of marriage was entered into for her with Charles of Spain, which was subsequently renounced in order that she might marry Louis XII. King of France. This ceremony was performed by proxy at Greenwich, on 14th of September, 1514, the Duke of Longueville representing King Louis. She was accompanied to France by a courtly retinue, and amongst her ladies was Anne Boleyn. The king met his bride at Abbeville, and the personal marriage was solemnized in the Cathedral. Mary was crowned at St. Denis on 5th of November, and from thence entered Paris in the midst of great demonstrations.

Louis was at this period in his fifty-third year, his young queen being only sixteen. At first she was greatly annoyed by the king's harsh dismissal of the greater portion of her retinue, but quickly forgot her vexation in the gaiety with which she was surrounded at the French Court. The king is said to have so far departed from his former early hours and quiet habits, in order to indulge her, as to have brought on the sickness and debility which caused his death on 1st of January, 1515, within three months of their union.

King Henry VIII. sent his favourite, Charles Brandon, afterwards created Duke of Suffolk, to condole with the young widow, and to arrange with the successor of Louis—

Francis I.—for the payment of the dowry of Mary. It is said that an attachment had grown up between Brandon and the princess prior to the arrangements for the marriage of the latter with the French king. The speedy renewal of this was the result of Brandon's embassy. Francis I. favoured the engagement, and even urged a clandestine marriage, as it suited his purpose to prevent the chance of Mary being married to a Spanish prince. Thus situated, Charles Brandon and the widowed queen were privately married immediately after the death of King Louis XII. Francis pleaded with Henry to forgive his sister and his favourite; and, after some show of opposition, they were received by the king, and the marriage was publicly solemnized at Greenwich on 16th of May, 1515.

Brandon had been twice previously married, so that the Princess Mary Tudor was his third wife. She became the mother of a son and two daughters. The son Henry died in his infancy. The eldest daughter, Frances, married Henry Grey, Marquis of Dorset, and the youngest, Eleanor, married Henry Clifford, Earl of Cumberland. The first named daughter, the Marchioness of Dorset, who became, after the death of Brandon and Mary, Duchess of Suffolk, was the mother of the beautiful and unfortunate Lady Jane Grey. It was as the grand-daughter and heiress of the sister of King Henry VIII. that the claim to the crown was set up on behalf of Lady Jane by her ambitious and unscrupulous relatives; a claim which ended in misfortune for herself and her youthful husband, Lord Guildford Dudley.

The Princess Mary died on the 25th of June, 1533, in her thirty-fifth year.

The authority for the portrait is a contemporary picture, painter unknown, in the possession of his grace the Duke of Bedford.

Charles Brandon,

DUKE OF SUFFOLK.

CHARLES BRANDON, the friend and companion in boyhood and youth of Henry VIII, and subsequently his successful general, and second husband of his sister Princess Mary, widow of Louis XII. of France, was the son of Sir William Brandon and Elizabeth Beuyn, daughter and co-heiress of Sir Henry Beuyn, who had previously married a gentleman named Mallory.

Sir William Brandon was a great supporter of the House of Lancaster, and had forfeited his estates under Richard III. Joining the Earl of Richmond in Britany, he landed with him on his return to England, and bore the standard of Lancaster at Bosworth Field, where he was killed by Richard himself, in the moment when victory had crowned the cause of the Lancastrians.

His son thus became the peculiar care of the King, Henry VII, and he was subsequently brought up with the royal family, attaching himself to Prince Henry, whose senior he must have been by some five or six years, at least.

On the accession of Henry VIII, he was appointed one of the Esquires of the Body, and Chamberlain of Wales: subsequently he was created Lord Lisle for his part in a naval action off Brest, in 1513. In June of that year he accompanied Henry in his invasion of France, and commanding the vanguard of the army, marched into Flanders.

In 1514 the Princess Mary, second sister of the king, was married to Louis XII. of France. The marriage was celebrated with great pomp, and Brandon is said to have distinguished himself so greatly in the tournament which was held on the occasion as to captivate the queen, although in all probability a strong affection had existed between them prior to this, which had to be set aside from political necessity. Louis XII. died within three months of his marriage, and a very few days after the queen married Charles Brandon secretly. King Henry made a show of resentment, but Brandon was too necessary a favourite for this to last long, and the angry mood ended in a grant of estates, which had belonged to Edmund de la Pole, Earl of Suffolk.

The marriage ceremony between Brandon and the king's sister was publicly performed at Greenwich, on 16th of May, 1515. On this occasion the bridegroom again distinguished himself in a tournament which formed a necessary part of the festivities on these occasions, and appeared with the following singular device, alluding to his new alliance :—

> Cloth of Gold do not despise,
> Though thou art matched with Cloth of Frieze,
> Cloth of Frieze be not too bold,
> Though thou art matched with Cloth of Gold.

Brandon was a singular example of the chivalry of the period, and his character for honour, integrity, courage, and straightforward dealing is testified on all hands. He was an able soldier and politician, and his abilities were devoted to the service of his king. He was created Duke of Suffolk by Edward VI. He died at Guildford, Surrey, on 14th of August, 1545, and was interred with great pomp, at the king's expense, in St. George's Chapel, Windsor, although by his will, in which he bequeaths a gold cup to the king, to be made out of his collar of the garter, he desired that his funeral should be conducted " without any pomp or outward pride of the world," and that he should be laid in the Collegiate Church, at Tatteshall, Lincolnshire.

Charles Brandon was married four times. His first wife was Margaret Nevile, widow of Sir John Mortimer, daughter of John Nevile, Marquis of Montacute. He moved for a divorce because he had previously signed a contract of marriage with Anne, daughter of Sir Anthony Brown, Lieutenant of Calais, whom he married for his second wife. Two daughters were born of this union. His third wife was Mary, Queen Dowager of France, sister of King Henry VIII, as already mentioned, who bore a son, Henry, created Earl of Lincoln, but who died young, and two daughters. The oldest was Frances, afterwards Marchioness of Dorset, and mother of Lady Jane Grey; the other, Eleanor, who married Henry Clifford, Earl of Cumberland. His fourth marriage was with Katherine, daughter and heiress of William, Lord Willoughby of Eresby. His two sons by this marriage, Henry and Charles, survived him only six years, as they both died of the " sweating sickness," at the Bishop of Lincoln's palace at Brigden, on 14th of July, 1551.

The authority used in painting this portrait is a contemporary picture, by an unknown painter, in the collection of the Duke of Bedford.

HE eldest daughter of the marriage between the younger sister of King Henry VIII, the Princess Mary, after the death of her first husband Louis XII. of France, and Charles Brandon, Duke of Suffolk, was the Lady Frances. She married Henry Grey, Marquis of Dorset, and after the death of Brandon, the title of Duke and Duchess of Suffolk was conferred upon them. Three daughters were born of this union, the eldest being the excellent and unfortunate Lady Jane Grey.

The weakness of character shown by Henry Grey made him a fit subject for aiding in the ambitious projects of the Duke of Northumberland, who affected to be so deeply attached to the Protestant faith as to consider it necessary to provide a Protestant successor to the young and sickly King Edward VI. As a preliminary step the three daughters of Frances Brandon were all married in one day—25th of May, 1553. Lady Jane Grey, as eldest daughter, and heiress of her grandmother Mary Tudor, was united to Lord Guildford Dudley, the eldest son of Northumberland; Lady Catherine Grey was married to Lord Herbert, son of the Earl of Pembroke, and Lady Mary Grey to Martin Keys, a groom of the king's chamber.

These marriages formed the groundwork of the plot of Northumberland to change the succession to the crown. The young and dying King Edward, influenced partly by a sincere desire for the religious welfare of his country, and partly by the persuasions of Northumberland, as well as affection for Lady Jane Grey, in whose scholarly pursuits he took great interest, wrote, some time in the beginning of June, with his own hand, " his device for the succession." In this document he left the crown to the heirs male of Lady Frances, or the heirs male of either of her three daughters; but a little later, and when he was really dying, he converted " the Lady Jane's heirs male," no doubt at the dictation of her husband's father, the Duke of Northumberland, into "the Lady Jane and her heirs male."* But as Lady Frances, then Duchess of Suffolk, was at that period only thirty-seven years old, might have a son, it was made a condition of the succession that such son should be born before Edward's death. This Northumberland well knew to be impossible.

After an appeal to the Lords, by the king's wish, to confirm this strange " device," and a personal appeal to the judges by the dying boy himself, the Lords rejected the settlement; and the judges declared it to be a legal impossibility.

Ultimately an arrangement was made with the council, Northumberland behaving in a most outrageous manner; but the judges adhered secretly to their opinion of the illegality of the proceedings.

Of course, after the death of Edward, this legality had to be tested, and the result was that Princess Mary, the eldest daughter of Henry VIII. by Katherine of Arragon, succeeded to the crown. Northumberland paid for his ambition with his head; but Henry Grey, Duke of Suffolk, though deeply implicated in the plot to secure the throne for his eldest daughter, Lady Jane Grey, was pardoned in 1553.

---

* See " Froude's History."

His weak but restless nature would not, however, allow him to rest content, and he took up arms with his brothers John and Leonard Grey, in Sir Thomas Wyatt's attempt to prevent the marriage of Queen Mary with Philip of Spain, in 1554. He was tried for this in Westminster Hall, on 17th of February, 1555, and beheaded on 23rd of February, eleven days after the execution of his daughter and her youthful husband.

Frances Marchioness of Dorset, and Duchess of Suffolk, was thus left a widow, and during the reign of Queen Mary lived in concealment, and it is said in poverty. This was changed on the accession of Elizabeth, who held her in much esteem. She married as her second husband Adrian Stokes, her Master of the Horse, and a country gentleman of considerable property.

It is related that when Queen Elizabeth heard of this marriage she remarked to her minister, Cecil, " So I hear that Suffolk has married her groom?" " Not her groom, please your highness, but her Master of the Horse," was the witty reply, for at that period Elizabeth had shown a strong inclination to marry the Earl of Leicester, who held the post of Master of the Horse to the queen. Cecil's ready answer is supposed to have had its effect upon Elizabeth, as, shortly after, the intention to marry Leicester was abandoned.

The Duchess of Suffolk died in December, 1559, and was buried in Westminster Abbey, where a tomb in alabaster, which still exists, was erected to her memory by her second husband, Adrian Stokes, or Stock, as inscribed thereon.

The authority for the portrait is a very fine picture by Lucas de Heere, in the possession of the Rev. Heneage Finch.

F

Lady Jane Grey.

ADY JANE GREY, whose character and melancholy end have been of so much interest to the people of England at all periods subsequent to that in which she lived, was the eldest daughter of Henry Grey, Marquis of Dorset, afterwards Duke of Suffolk, and Lady Frances, daughter of Charles Brandon, Duke of Suffolk, and his royal consort, Mary, youngest sister of Henry VIII, widow of Louis XII. of France. She was born in 1537, and was a remarkable exception to the ladies of her time, alike in her character and her pursuits. Her education was entrusted to a Protestant clergyman, John Aylmer, afterwards Bishop of London during the reign of Queen Elizabeth.

Her parents appear to have treated her in a very imperious manner, and thus attached her so much the more to her amiable and able tutor, and the pursuits of literature. Her knowledge of languages was very remarkable; whilst she excelled in all the usual female accomplishments of her time. Fuller says of her:—" She had the innocence of childhood, the beauty of youth, the solidity of middle, and the gravity of old age; and all at eighteen. The birth of a princess, the learning of a clerk, the life of a saint, and the death of a malefactor for her parents' offences."

Without complicity on her part, she was made the head of a political faction in the reign of Edward VI, whose deli-

LADY J·GREY

cacy of constitution led those about him to anticipate his early death. Dudley, Duke of Northumberland, having succeeded in bringing about the fall of the Protector Somerset, the guardian of the young king, negotiated a marriage between his son Guildford Dudley and Lady Jane Grey, which took place on 25th of May, 1553; and absurdly supposed that, in the event of the death of Edward VI, he could claim the crown for them through the royal descent of his daughter-in-law. He thus ignored the legal claims of the Princess Mary and the Princess Elizabeth, daughters of Henry VIII, for the suppositious right of Lady Jane, who was simply the descendant of the second sister of Henry;— her own mother, the Marchioness of Dorset, now Duchess of Suffolk, being still living.

Relying upon his power, his influence over the young king, and the affection with which Edward regarded Lady Jane Grey from similarity of talents, disposition, and pursuits, the wily Northumberland induced the king to prepare with his own hand a document practically settling the succession on his youthful cousin. The terms were, after much difficulty, apparently sanctioned by the Privy Council; but declared illegal by the judges. Northumberland meeting with opposition from the Chief Justice of the Common Pleas, Sir Edward Montague, was roused to such a fury as to declare in the Council Chamber that he would " fight any man in his shirt " who attempted to interfere with the king's wishes. After much opposition on the part of the judges and others, the letters patent, as they were called, were finally signed by Edward on 21st of June, 1553. On 6th of July he died.

The fatal ambition of her own and her husband's kindred resulted in a temporary elevation to the throne; but she only yielded consent when urged by her mother, the Duchess of

Suffolk, (as the Marchioness of Dorset was now called), and her youthful and inexperienced husband. She was proclaimed queen on 10th of July, her own mother having borne her train as she entered the Tower of London in royal state. The members of the Council of State, under the guidance of Suffolk, were practically prisoners in the Tower, so doubtful was Northumberland of their faithfulness; for as the Princess Mary had demanded the crown, and actually been proclaimed in some parts of the country, the Council became uneasy, well knowing the illegality of the articles they had consented to. Ultimately, by pretending great devotion to the cause of Lady Jane Grey, and a desire to raise troops to defend her right to the throne against the army already organizing for Mary, they were permitted to leave the Tower, and once at liberty, they declared for Queen Mary, whom they proclaimed in London on 19th of July, 1553.

Lady Jane Grey at once bowed to the necessities of her position with characteristic amiability. She reminded her father how unwilling she had been to take the position forced upon her, and sought to show that by giving up at once all the claims which had been put forth on her behalf, those who had been her supporters might hope to extenuate their fault. Through the influence of her mother with the queen, Suffolk, her father, was pardoned; but, by a strange infatuation, he, with his two brothers, mixed themselves up with Sir Thomas Wyatt's rebellion; and, though there is every reason to believe that Mary had intended to spare the life of the innocent victim of family ambition, the fact that the powerful house of Grey had again arrayed itself against her, made clemency almost impossible, and the death of the young husband and wife was determined on, although it is now understood that Queen Mary confirmed the decision with great reluctance.

On 12th of February, 1554, she was beheaded in the Tower, having previously seen her husband, Lord Guildford Dudley, pass to the scaffold, and witnessed the return of his lifeless body.

The authorities used in executing the portrait were a picture in the collection of Earl Spencer, and an engraving in Hodge's portraits, after a picture in the possession of the Earl of Stamford and Warrington.

Lord Guildford Dudley.

GUILDFORD DUDLEY was the third son of Sir John Dudley, created Earl of Warwick in 1547, and subsequently Duke of Northumberland, and Jane Guildford, only daughter of Sir Edward Guildford. He was only remarkable for his misfortune in having been the son of so ambitious a father, since it was through his marriage, in May, 1553, with Lady Jane Grey, that Northumberland hoped to secure for his son the position of consort to the successor of Edward VI.

Lord Guildford Dudley appears to have fallen in with the lofty schemes of his father and the Duke of Suffolk, and paid for his indiscretion with his life. He was beheaded on 12th of February, 1554, at the Tower of London; having preceded his young and admirable wife to that scaffold from which she saw his dead body carried back. It is recorded that she then wrote three brief passages in three languages. That in Greek was:—"If his slain body shall give testimony against me before men, his blessed soul shall receive an eternal proof of my innocence before God." The one in Latin reads:—"The justice of men took away his body, but the Divine mercy has preserved his soul." The third was in English:—"If my fault deserved punishment, my youth and my imprudence were worthy of excuse." ·

The authority for the portrait is a picture in the possession of Col. North, M.P.

James the Fourth, of Scotland.

AMES IV. was the son of James III. of Scotland, and Princess Margaret of Denmark, daughter of Christian, King of Denmark.

His conduct as heir apparent to the throne was most undutiful. He allowed himself to be influenced by a party of discontented nobles, and then headed them in open rebellion against the king. Having been pardoned with all his followers, after dictating his own terms, he again rose in arms against the authority of his father, who, unfortunately, instead of awaiting the arrival of his trusty friends, the northern lords of his kingdom, assembled an army and attacked the prince and his followers at Sauchieburn, near Bannockburn. The king's forces being inferior in numbers were defeated, and James III. lost his life, by the hand of an assassin, in his thirty-fifth year, at the little village of Milltoun, on 18th of June, 1488.

His ungrateful son and successor, James IV, is said to have evinced great remorse when informed of the death of the king; but this feeling seems to have soon passed away. He was crowned at the Abbey of Scone, on 24th of June, 1488, and was then in his seventeenth year. His character at this age appears to have been marked with more than ordinary force, so that he could not have been, as has been stated, a mere instrument in the hands of a faction.

The successful treason of the new king and his followers led to their acquittal by the parliament, and the condemnation of the loyal nobles who had borne arms in defence of

their late sovereign. An attempt on their part to avenge
the death of the king, in which they hoisted the blood-stained
shirt of the unfortunate monarch on a spear as a banner,
was speedily suppressed; and this rising, and its suppression,
only gave strength to the young king and his party.

He made peace with Henry VII. of England, and, with
the exception of a short period in which he identified himself
with the pretender to the English throne, Perkin Warbeck,
who took refuge in Scotland in 1495, tranquillity with England was preserved for twenty years.   In this effort against
Henry VII, the purpose of which it is difficult to understand,
James did not display his usual ability. Instigated in the
attempt by the Duchess of Burgundy, probably without believing Warbeck's claims, the Scottish king invaded Northumberland, and carried on war after such a brutal fashion
that he soon found the English had no sympathy with the
cause of the pretender, and that even those who were
opposed to Henry were disgusted with the manner in which
their Scottish friends carried out that opposition. Finding
so little sympathy with this invasion, James negotiated a
truce, which ended in a treaty of peace. This was in
1497, and in 1502 this amicable understanding with the
English monarch resulted in James espousing the eldest
daughter of Henry VII, the Princess Margaret of England,
—the passage of the princess to Scotland, and the celebration of the marriage on 8th of August, 1503, being conducted with great pomp and magnificence.

Prior to the rupture with England, thus happily healed,
James had shown great capacity as a ruler. The Highlands
of Scotland, from whence his father's best friends had come
remained in a constant state of incipient insurrection. He
visited these northern districts of his kingdom, twice in
1490, and twice again in 1493. In 1494 he visited the

isles three times; on one occasion in great state, with a considerable fleet. The chiefs were thus impressed with the power of their young king, and he succeeded in assimilating the laws and lax administration of justice in those wild regions, to something more in accordance with the southern modes of civil and criminal procedure, instead of leaving this important department of government to the caprice and tyrannical notions of the rude nobles and heads of clans.

In former reigns the nobility and court were invariably separated. The king and the most powerful of his subjects, alike for good or evil, had comparatively little intercourse. Hence the terrible scenes of revolt and murder which characterize early Scottish history. James early sought to change this. Fond of society and magnificence, or courteous manners, he surrounded himself by those whose wealth and position could assist him in the formation of a brilliant court. There was a subtle under-current of policy in this; for as the extravagance they were led to indulge in rendered the nobles poor, so they became more and more dependent upon the grace and favour of the king. The retirement, too, of their own estates, and the residences they were compelled to live in, the strongholds of a former age, became distasteful to them: therefore these were neglected, and with them that cultivation of personal intercourse with their retainers which had led, in former times, to so much devotion and zeal in the time of revolt against the kingly authority.

James, too, turned his attention to the development of a navy; encouraged the fisheries; treated merchants and such manufacturers as showed skill and aptitude in their callings with great consideration. Nor did he shrink from personal experiment and sacrifices to encourage and understand all matters which his quick perception led him to believe would be useful to his country. He made himself familiar

with the details of shipbuilding and navigation, as also of
gunnery, and induced many able foreigners to settle in Scotland. He was, no doubt, greatly imposed upon at times,
but this was compensated for by solid results in other direc-
tions. He encouraged learning by assisting Elphinstone,
Bishop of Aberdeen, to found the University of Aberdeen,
in 1494, although the building subsequently known as
"King's College," was not completed until 1500.

So long as Henry VII. of England lived, James seems to
have been prosperous. In 1505 an insurrection of the High-
land chiefs occupied him ;—the object being to reinstate
the grandson of the Lord of the Isles, who had unsuccess-
fully defied the power of James in 1494, in his sovereignty
over the insular portions of the kingdom. Having accomplished the suppression of this revolt, he divided these districts into two new sheriffdoms, and garrisoned the castles
with his troops, and finally produced the desired change in
the manner and habits of the people, by inducing them to
abandon their habits of plunder, and pay respect to the laws.

The accession of Henry VIII. to the throne of England,
in 1509, was the beginning of much anxiety and trouble to
James and his kingdom. The overbearing character of
Henry was calculated to irritate the proud and high-spirited
James, although for a time all went more agreeably than
might have been expected. Complications, however, came
at last. Henry declared war against France, the ancient
ally of Scotland, and James, with that chivalry for which he
was distinguished, declared against his brother-in-law, and
the true interests of Scotland, by taking sides with the
French king, who, hoping to embarrass Henry, induced
James to declare war against England. This uncalled-for
and foolish step was fatal to the Scottish king and Scotland.
His very popularity made it the more dangerous for his

people, since they at once rallied round him on an appeal to arms, and the result was an array of force, by sea and land, which Scotland had never mustered on any previous occasion. The naval force was intended to invade Ireland; but being commanded by the Earl of Arran, his inexperience in maritime tactics led to its overthrow. The king in person took command of the army, amounting to nearly one hundred thousand men. Marching through the border Cheviots, he encamped his army in a strong position at Flodden. Henry of England had gone to France with his army, but had given the command of the troops sent against the Scotch to the Earl of Surrey, who, with a force not amounting to half that of the Scottish army, crossed the river Till, which formed the defence of James's front, and attacked him. The Scottish king seems to have been infatuated with some notions of chivalry and dependence on personal courage, rather than on strategy, and the importance of making the best use of his position and numbers. In spite of all remonstrance he would not allow any of his veterans, such as Angus, Huntley, or Lindsey, to attack Surrey until all the English had passed the river; even his artillery, under Borthwick, was silent, although he had, with marvellous acuteness, foreseen the value of this portion of an armed force, and had sedulously encouraged its development for several years, at great cost. The end, of course, came all too soon. Surrey, having passed the bridge and ford, marshalled his army, and placing himself between James and his dominions, attacked the Scottish army in the rear. The king's fanciful array of his forces into five portions was useless, when attacked by the English in two divisions only. The onslaught was made at four in the afternoon of 6th of September, 1513, and continued until night. The total defeat of the Scots was the result, and scarcely a family of any note in the whole land but had to mourn the loss of some member.   The king fought with a desperate courage, and his body was found surrounded by the bodies of his nobles, who had preferred death in his defence to dishonour on any other terms.

Such was the end, in his forty-second year, of James IV. of Scotland ; a monarch whose reign, though commenced, as it ended, in violence, was still of immense value to the country over which he reigned.   Notwithstanding his un-dutiful behaviour to his father, he appears to have been naturally kind-hearted; and taking a deep interest in the wel-fare of his subjects, as he understood it, he was easily acces-sible to all.   Fond of improvement, he promoted agriculture, commerce, manufactures, and the peaceful arts, as well as those of war.   Printing was introduced into Scotland in 1509, and greatly encouraged by him.   His ambition and love of military glory, and his obstinate adherence to his own personal notions of individual honour, cost him his life, and brought misery upon his subjects and his family.

The authorities from which the portrait was executed are several old and scarce engravings.

Princess Margaret.

HE Princess Margaret was the eldest daughter of King Henry VII. and Elizabeth Woodville, daughter of Edward IV. The best authorities fix the date of her birth as 29th of November, 1489. From motives of policy the king, her father, decided to offer her in marriage to James IV. of Scotland, while she was yet an infant, as he wished to detach that brave and chivalrous prince from the party of the Duchess of Burgundy, sister of Edward IV, who had put forth Perkin Warbeck as a pretender to the crown of England. This offer was made before the princess was six years old.

James, however, refused the bribe, and invaded England, having Perkin Warbeck with him. Subsequently, through that system of intrigue which characterized the policy of Henry, the two kings pledged themselves to friendship, and James accepted the offer of Henry, and on St. Paul's-day, January, 1502, Margaret was married by proxy at Richmond;—Patrick, Earl of Bothwell, representing James. Great festivities followed, and on 27th of June, the young queen commenced her progress to Scotland.

Leland gives a very quaint and interesting account of the doings on this occasion.* As riding in carriages was not

---

* Leland's "De Rebus Anglicanis Opuscula Varia."

yet the fashion, since carriages worth riding in had to be invented, Leland says :—" The Qwene was richly drest, mounted on a faire Palfrey, and before her rode Sir Davy Owen during all the sayde voyage richly appoynted. Thre Fotemen wer alwayes ny hyr varey honestly appoynted and had in their Jaketts browdered Portecollys." As a means of making a more dignified and lady-like display when appearing before the people assembled in the cities through which she passed, a litter was provided, " in which the sayde Qwene was born in the Intrying of the goods Tounes or otherways to her good Playsur."

Margaret was accompanied by knights and ladies selected by the king, her father, who relieved each other in relays as she passed from one district to another, and she was met by the nobility, and entertained by them and corporations,—municipal and religious. She arrived at Berwick-on-Tweed on 29th, and remained there on 30th and 31st of July, leaving for her entry into Scotland on 1st of August. On 3rd of that month King James met her near Haddington, at a castle belonging to the Earl of Morton. Here the king seems to have frequently visited his bride up to the day on which the marriage took place at Edinburgh—8th of August, 1503, amidst a gorgeous display of festivity and splendour.

James was in his thirty-second year, and Margaret in her fourteenth. They appear to have lived together very happily, the king treating his girl-wife with much consideration, and a mutual affection eventually existed between them. The death of Henry VII, in 1509, was the forerunner of misfortunes to both.

Henry VIII. renewed the friendly compact entered into by his father, and kept it for two years ; but discords sprang up in which Henry's overbearing policy, met as it was by the impetuous nature of the Scottish king, led to an open rupture. War was the result, and James IV. fell at the battle of Flodden Field, on 9th of September, 1513. Queen Margaret was thus left a widow with an only son, James, as the successor of his able, popular, and chivalrous father. This child was very little more than a twelvemonth old ; and his mother was appointed regent by the will of his father. She was then in the twenty-fourth year of her age. Her second son, Alexander, was born after the death of the king, and was created Duke of Ross, but died before he was two years old. Immediately after his birth, to the surprise and regret of her subjects, she married Archibald Douglas, Earl of Angus, whose chief recommendation was his personal appearance.

A party was formed to supersede the queen in the regency; and as her authority was unaided by her brother, King Henry VIII, it succeeded; and John Stuart, Duke of Albany, first cousin to the late King James, and heir-presumptive to the crown, became regent. Henry evidently hoped that intestine feuds would bring Scotland within his grasp, and he did nothing for his sister except give advice, which, if followed, would have led to this result.

Albany reached Scotland in 1515, and treated Queen Margaret with great harshness, and, through the Parliament, demanded possession of her children. A deputation of peers waited upon her for this purpose; she received them at the gate of Edinburgh Castle, holding the young king by the hand, his baby brother being in the nurse's arms. When the lords came up to the gate, she demanded the cause of their coming, and on learning it, commanded the instant fall of the portcullis, and, defying their authority, asked six days to consider the proposal. Her daring spirit did not serve her, for the cowardly Angus tried to make his peace with Albany, by declaring that he had urged the queen to comply with the wishes of the regent, and surrender the children. Subsequently Margaret retired to Stirling Castle, taking her children with her. The regent besieged it with seven thousand men, and eventually forced the young king and his infant brother from the arms of their mother; and she was then conducted back to Edinburgh. Angus fled into his own part of the country. Margaret, a victim to force, fraud, and her own folly, had to return to England. Angus accompanied her by permission of Henry, angry though the latter was at her union with him. Eight days after her arrival in England, in October, 1515, she gave birth to a daughter at Harbottle, in Northumberland. This child, her daughter Margaret, afterwards married Matthew Stuart, Earl of Lennox, and became the mother of a line of kings; and that line remains to this day: for the son of Margaret Douglas and Matthew Stuart—Henry, Lord Darnley—became the second husband of Mary Queen of Scots, and father of James I. of England. In acute suffering Queen Margaret reached Morpeth; but illness prevented further progress southward. Here the faithless Angus left her to make his peace with the Regent Albany—an act of cruelty for which she never forgave him. It was in April, 1516, when she reached her brother's court. After almost constant turmoil in the midst of the intrigues of Henry, Albany, and Angus, she returned to Scotland, and again assumed, practically, the head of affairs. Forgetful of her dignity, she committed many foolish and wicked acts; endeavouring to obtain a divorce from Angus, out of love for her old enemy Albany, she finally formed an attachment to Henry Stuart, second son of Lord Evandale, whom she actually created, although a mere boy, Lord Treasurer and Chancellor of Scotland. Finally, she obtained the divorce from Angus in 1525, and then married Stuart, her son, King James V, creating him

Lord Methven. Ultimately, popular favourite though she had been, Margaret Tudor fell into contempt with her people, from her domestic follies and political intrigues ; and having lost all influence, even with her son, she retired to die at Methven, in June, 1541, and was buried in the church of the Carthusians at Perth.

The authority from which the portrait was executed is a picture in the collection of the Marquis of Lothian.

Douglas, Earl of Angus.

ARCHIBALD DOUGLAS was the sixth Earl of Angus, the head of the second branch of the great house of Douglas, and grandson of the famous Earl " Bell the Cat."

With a handsome person, he was active, brave, and ambitious. Impetuous and reckless in his conduct, it seems almost incredible that Queen Margaret could have selected him for her second husband, so soon after the death of King James IV ; and there can be no doubt that in doing so she sunk in the esteem of those of her subjects who could better appreciate the character of Angus, as a violent, headstrong, and unprincipled noble, in all matters in which his own interests, or those of his family, were concerned.

Possibly the queen thought that the whole power of the house of Douglas would be brought against the claims of Albany to become the regent of the kingdom during her infant son's minority. In this she was not disappointed, but the result must have been very far from being in accordance with her wishes and expectations.

Angus proved a faithless, and in all probability, a brutal husband. Several years her junior, he seems only to have cared for her so far as his own ambitious and personal objects were concerned.

After the infant king, and his younger brother Alexander,

had been placed under the care of the Regent Albany, Margaret had to fly to England for safety; and it was on this occasion she gave birth to the daughter born of the marriage with Angus, afterwards known as the Lady Margaret Douglas; who subsequently married Matthew Stuart, Earl of Lennox, and was the mother of Henry, Lord Darnley, the second husband of Mary Queen of Scots.

In 1516, Angus had leagued himself with Lord Home; but the latter, falling into the hands of Albany, was beheaded. Albany, reared in France, disliked Scotland as a residence, and on obtaining the permission of the Estates to visit France, handed over his power as regent to a council, of which Angus got named as a member. This led to the return of the queen, with all due honour, and things promised to go on more smoothly. The Earl of Arran, however, as head of the house of Hamilton, but who had played fast and loose with the Regent Albany, opposed the influence of Angus and the house of Douglas, and, of course, fierce dissensions followed. In January, 1520, Angus appeared at the parliament held at Edinburgh, with four hundred armed retainers; Arran, mustering the Hamiltons in even greater numbers, prepared to oppose force to force. The Bishop of Dunkeld, Gawin Douglas, a son of " Bell the Cat," endeavoured to make peace, and went to the Chancellor Beaton, Archbishop of Glasgow, a partisan of Arran's, to get him to use his influence with the Hamiltons. Beaton protested that he wished for peace, but could not prevent the collision about to take place, and in doing so laid his hand upon his heart; but Gawin Douglas was not to be deceived, and as he heard chain armour ring under the bishop's rochet, he told Beaton, " Ha! my lord, methinks your conscience clatters!" The end was a terrific battle in the streets of Edinburgh, known afterwards as " Cleanse the Causeway," between the Douglases and the Hamiltons, in which the former were victorious, and Angus was thus elevated for a period to the head of affairs.

The queen, however, had discovered her error in marrying him, and her aversion for him was such that she joined the party who desired the return of Albany, which took place on 3rd of December, 1521. Angus saw at once that his power was gone, and retired to England to avoid the fate of Home. Here he played into the hands of Henry VIII, whose army invaded Scotland under Surrey, during another absence of Albany in France. After an attempt to repel the English, by returning to Scotland and getting together a suitable force, the regent abandoned his task and the attempt to preserve his power as governor of the young king. He finally quitted Scotland, execrated by the people, whom he had impoverished by his extravagance and incapacity.

James V. being now twelve years old was declared by his mother, Queen Margaret, as henceforth the sovereign power in the realm, and the nobles rallied round her and the young king. Of course, English interests lay at the bottom of all this, or rather Henry VIII. and Wolsey sought to govern Scotland through Queen Margaret, and in the name of her son. To this end a reconciliation was proposed between Angus and Margaret. The latter, however, would not listen to any proposal which would reinstate Angus in power, or even allow him to return to Scotland; for, in addition to her resentment against him, she had become fascinated with the youthful Henry Stuart, and hoping to get rid of Angus by a divorce, had no doubt even then resolved to marry this new object of her passions.

Henry VIII, disappointed in obtaining a complete ascendancy in Scottish affairs through reuniting Angus and his sister, showed his disapproval of her conduct by doing all he could to assist Douglas in obtaining the superior power in spite of the queen. So supported, Angus resolved to destroy the power of his wife, since she would not share it with him, and a struggle commenced in which, after an attempt to take Edinburgh by escalade, and a union with the unscrupulous Archbishop Beaton, the Douglas party, headed by Angus, was successful. The young king, then fourteen years old, was committed to the care of a council of nobles, with the queen mother to preside at their consultations. She had, however, the appearance of power without the reality; since Angus had managed, by great attention to the young king, to influence him so greatly as to obtain a complete ascendancy over him. Angus, however, endeavoured to propitiate Queen Margaret by no longer opposing her efforts to obtain a divorce, which, when successful, ended by her marriage with Henry Stuart.

Had Angus shown the same sagacity in the use of his power as he had in obtaining it, he might have been a benefactor to his country, and a father to the young king; but he had no notion of using power for any other purpose than personal aggrandizement, and the promotion of the interest of his family and faction. Of course, injustice and oppression bore their usual fruit, and the young king himself felt the iron power of the Douglas chiefs; for Angus was influenced by his brother, Sir George Douglas, a haughty, hot-headed partisan.

Archbishop Beaton, the queen mother, and many of the nobles were opposed to the Douglas party, and many attempts were made to obtain possession of the person of the young king. Battles were fought, in which Angus was usually victorious; but in the end James managed to escape from his keepers, and the power of Angus was at an end.

After an abortive effort to regain possession of the king's· person, and the authority which acting in his name had conferred upon them, the Douglases found it necessary to retreat into England, and place themselves under the pro· tection of Henry VIII, for the parliament summoned Angus and his followers to answer for their abuse of the king's authority, and to obey this summons was practically to seek destruction ; since lawful defence was impossible. Angus, however, was not the man to retire without a struggle, so he put a garrison into Tantallon Castle, and took the field against the authorities, defying the king with such success that James had to retreat from the siege of the castle, his army being attacked in the rear by Angus ; who added to his other delinquencies against the king by killing David Falconer, a favourite officer of James'. This still further increased the resentment of the young monarch, who swore that no Douglas should, so long as he lived, exercise any power in Scotland. Finding all his efforts useless, Angus, as already stated, sought refuge in England, hoping that Henry's influence or power could eventually produce some result on his obdurate nephew.

In 1542, Angus and his partisans made another attempt to return to Scotland. Henry VIII. having declared war against his nephew, James V, an army was sent to the borders. This was met at Haddon-rig by the Scots, under the command of the Earl of Huntley, and the English were defeated. Angus barely saved himself by using his dagger upon the knight who attempted to take him prisoner.

On the death of James V, after the rout of the Solway, Angus and his brother, Sir George Douglas, the father of the Regent Morton, returned to Scotland without waiting for pardon or invitation, and immediately after ; the forfeiture of their estates was reversed by the parliament. Their long residence in England under the protection of Henry led that monarch to expect some return for his hospitality, and he sought to use the Douglases to serve the interests of the English party in obtaining a contract of marriage between the infant Mary Stuart and his son Edward, Prince of Wales, afterwards Edward VI ; but he was too impatient, and ultimately had again to invade Scotland. This was done after such a reckless and cruel fashion that even Angus, his brother-in-law and pensioner, felt compelled to take the field against him, and gave such efficient help in avenging the ravages committed, that when Lord Ewers and Sir Brian Latoun advanced into the borders of Teviotdale to take *saisin* of certain lordships there, Angus hurled defiance at Henry and said, " I will write them an instrument of investiture with sharp pens and bloody ink ;" since he found that a large portion of his own estate was included in Henry's grant to the English proprietors.

The defeat of the English in the battle of Jedburgh, after the sacking of Melrose Abbey, in which the tombs of the Douglases were wantonly injured, filled the cup of Angus with Henry, and the latter vowed vengeance on the Scottish earl for his ingratitude. Douglas, however, was coolly defiant, and wrote—" Is our brother angry that I have avenged on Ralph Ewers the injury done to the tombs of my ancestors ? They were better men than he, and I could in honour do no less. And will he take my life for that ? Little knows King Henry the heights of Cairntable.* I can keep myself safe there against the power of England."

Henry's spirit against Scotland seems to have animated the Protector Somerset, for after his death the English made another attempt to subdue the southern borders. At the

---

* Cairntable, a mountain in Douglas dale.

battle of Pinkie, which ended so disastrously for the Scots, Angus commanded the vanguard. In seeking to change the position of his troops, so as to avoid the effects of the English cannon, he communicated a panic to the Scottish army, which, from the retrograde character of the movement, fancied the front had given way. The English Earl of Warwick took advantage of this, and dashing in with his cavalry before the Scots could re-form, a total rout was the consequence.

From this time Angus seems to have practically slipped out of sight, and almost the last record in history of his public life is that in which we are told of his characteristic reply to Mary of Guise, when she wished to garrison his castle of Tantallon with French soldiers. "Tantallon," said Angus, "is at your majesty's command as regent of the kingdom, but, by St. Bride of Douglas, I must remain castellan of the fortress for your behoof, and I will keep it better for you than any foreigners you can place there."

The authority for the portrait is a picture in the Royal Collection at Windsor Castle.

James the Fifth, of Scotland.

AMES V. was the eldest son of James IV. and his queen, Margaret Tudor, daughter of King Henry VII. At the period of his father's death, at the battle of Flodden Field, he was a child in his sixth year, and his younger brother, Alexander, Duke of Ross, was born after that unfortunate event.

His mother's hasty and indecorous marriage with Archibald Douglas, Earl of Angus, led to serious complications respecting the regency, which was finally settled, for a time at least, in the hands of the Duke of Albany. The French predilections of the Regent, however, were disagreeable to the majority of the Scottish nobles, and he soon returned to France; anarchy prevailing in the government, and the northern part of the kingdom and Isles. Angus deserted the queen, and joined the English party, as it was called, for it worked into the hands of King Henry VIII. In the struggle that ensued, the Douglases and Angus were successful; but Albany returned from France after the murder of De la Bastie, whom he had named deputy-governor and lord warden of the marches, and Angus fled from the capital. The queen then became reconciled to Albany as regent, and he took charge of the young king. Angus did not return until 1524, after which he again became a lord of misrule. Leagued with the other Douglases, they eventually obtained possession of the person of the boy king, and continued to hold all the power in the State.

When James became old enough to appreciate his position, he naturally enough hated Angus and all his family. In his seventeenth year he had learned dissimulation enough to put on the appearance of contentment, in order to allay the suspicions of his keepers ; and, taking advantage of the absence of Angus and others, he made his escape one night from their custody, in the garb of a yeoman of the stable busy with the preparation for the next day's hunting ; and, mounting a horse, rode, accompanied by two servants, to Stirling Castle.

Summoning a council, he declared it treason in Angus, or any Douglas, to approach within six miles of his court. Deprived of the power to act in the king's name, Angus and his party contemplated an attack on Stirling Castle ; but the declaration of the king, which was made known to them by a herald who met them on the way, caused them to return.

The character of James was at this period at once vigorous, and in advance of his years. His training had been severe, and he had been constantly under restraint as to the manifestation of his own will. Intellectually, too, he had not been neglected ; but the Douglases had cunningly encouraged him in a love of pleasure, as by that means they hoped to disincline him to useful pursuits, or active interference with questions of government. His native energy, however, though modified, was not subdued, and there was in him much of good. He loved justice, though by no means merciful ; he disliked oppression, especially of the weak. He had little personal pride, and was accessible to all ; and thus he was liked by the nobles, and was a favourite with the people. His hatred of the Douglases was intense, and was the dominant feeling of his life. His jealousy of foreign dictation, of which he saw the evil results, brought him into secret antagonism with his uncle, King Henry VIII, but endeared him to the Scots.

Seeking to limit the power of the nobles, he gave important posts of State to the clergy, and encouraged the mercantile and commercial classes to assert their rights. In 1535 he developed a reformation of the corporation system, that great help to freedom in the middle ages ; and the posts of magistrates were no longer to be considered as appanage of the factious and tyrannical amongst the nobility. Treason in many shapes lifted itself up against his authority, and the Douglas adherents were constantly aiming at producing a rupture with England. A principal border leader, the Earl of Bothwell, made a treaty with Henry VIII, in which he undertook to dethrone James, and Angus took the oath of allegiance to the English king. The ability and firmness of James, supported however by the whole power of his people, finally prevailed, and a treaty of peace was made for the period of the lives of the two kings. James was now in his twenty-second year, and his courage and talent were recognized on all hands. He received the order of the Golden Fleece from the emperor, St. Michael from France, and, above all, the Garter from England.

In 1536 he married, at Notre Dame, Paris, the Princess Madelaine, the daughter of the Duke of Vendôme ; and, after a stay of nine months in France for the purpose of accomplishing this object of his marriage without giving offence to Henry VIII, whose daughter Mary had been proposed to him, he returned to Scotland, but only to see his young queen waste away and die of consumption, almost as soon as the rejoicings of his people, in celebration of the wedding, were over. Within a year he married Mary of Guise, the widow of the Duke of Longueville, and sister to Cardinal Lorraine. The ceremony was performed at St. Andrews, in 1537. It was about this time the Douglas family are said to have organized two attempts on the king's life, and two of the relatives of Angus were executed.

For some years the great principles of the Reformation had been making way in Scotland in spite of some severe examples. Patrick Hamilton, Abbot of Ferne, the disciple and friend of Luther, was burnt at St. Andrews, for heresy, in 1528; others also suffered in 1534. Henry VIII. had endeavoured to convert James to his views of independence of the Church of Rome; but James was not likely to follow the example of such a leader.

The marriage of James with Mary of Guise, who, like all her family, was an ardent supporter of the authority of the Church of Rome, together with Henry's intrigues while James was away in France, only served to confirm the Scottish king in his allegiance to the Pope; and he left ecclesiastical affairs in the hands of Cardinal Beaton, who had, unhappily, a great influence over him. The result was a most inhuman treatment of the Reformers, and especially of the minor clergy.

James busied himself with the secular affairs of his kingdom, visited the northern parts of his dominions in great state, and sought to develope a navy. The nobles, however, still kept aloof, and plotted against his life; and he despaired of uniting all interests for the welfare of Scotland. He granted an amnesty to all offenders except Angus, Sir George Douglas, and their partisans.

James was not uninfluenced by the reforming tendencies of the age. The great hope of the leaders of the Roman episcopacy, led by Cardinal Beaton, was a war with England. King Henry, however, was anxious to bring his nephew to declare against the see of Rome, and proposed an interview at York. James did not keep the appointment, and this precipitated a war, which was declared against Scotland in 1542. James was greatly depressed at this time by the death of his two infant sons, Arthur and James; he was poor, too, and by no means sure of the fidelity of his nobles. With an army of 30,000 men he advanced, and reached Fala Moor. Norfolk, the English commander, had to retire for want of supplies, and from the severity of the winter. James at once resolved to retaliate, and invade England; but the nobles, as he feared, failed to support him in an invasion, and he had to return to his capital, humiliated by his own people. That King James felt all this very severely cannot be doubted; and he became timid and distrustful of those about him. Another army of 10,000 men was got together, under Lord Maxwell; and James stationing himself at Caerlaverock to await the result of the expedition. It was unsuccessful, and shamefully so, for James, being distrustful of Maxwell, gave the command to his favourite, Oliver Sinclair, and, in the midst of the contention which ensued, the English horse, about three hundred strong, advanced to reconnoitre, and, seeing the condition of things, at once charged upon the Scots, and utterly routed them.

James, overwhelmed by this final calamity, and wounded in spirit, refused to be comforted. He became silently melancholy, and, while in this state, and practically dying, the news of the birth of a daughter, afterwards the beautiful and unfortunate Mary Queen of Scots, reached him. Here was another disappointment, for he had hoped for a son to replace "those gone before." In the very spirit of despair,

he exclaimed, " It came wi' a lass, it will gang wi' a lass,"
alluding to the crown of Scotland having come to his
ancestor, Walter the Steward, by his marriage with Margery
Bruce, only daughter of King Robert Bruce. These were
almost his last words, for, taking an affectionate farewell of
his followers, after giving them his hand to kiss, he quickly
closed his eyes in death.

James V. was in the thirty-fifth year of his age, and the
twenty-ninth of his reign when he died, leaving another
long minority as a legacy to his country.

The authority from which the portrait was executed is a
picture in the collection of his grace the Duke of Devonshire.

Mary of Guise.

ARY OF LORRAINE was a daughter of the Duke of Guise, and sister of the Cardinal of Lorraine. She first married the Duke of Longueville, and was a widow when James V. of Scotland proposed for her hand after the death of his first queen, Madelaine of Bourbon. The marriage ceremony was celebrated at St. Andrews, in 1537. She bore two sons, Arthur and James; and the early death of these young princes had a very depressing effect on the mind of the king. Her third child, Mary, afterwards so celebrated as Queen of Scots, was born only eight days before the death of King James, after the rout at Solway Moss; and as queen mother, Mary of Guise became the practical head of the state, around whom the great body of the more dignified clergy, headed by Cardinal Beaton, and the Roman Catholic nobility, rallied. The Earl of Arran, the representative of the house of Hamilton, as the next heir to the throne, and who leaned to the opinions of the Reformation, headed a strong party in the State; and was eventually chosen governor of the realm, and guardian to the baby queen.

Hatred of Cardinal Beaton and the Church of Rome led this party to play into the hands of Henry VIII. of England, and assist his intrigues to obtain a pledge of an alliance between the infant Queen of Scotland and his son, afterwards

Edward VI. The French party, however, led by Mary of Guise the queen mother, prevailed. Henry, being foiled, declared war against Scotland, which he carried on after so cruel a fashion that his own brother-in-law and partisan, Angus, was ashamed, especially when he found his own border estates were involved in the proposed confiscation. Henry's invasion came to a sudden end at the battle of Ancrum Moor in 1544, when Angus and another Douglas, uniting with the forces of the regent, attacked the English and utterly routed them.

This victory, although due more to vengeance than to patriotism, helped to restore confidence in Scotland. The brutal assassination of Cardinal Beaton, instigated, it is said, by Henry, soon followed; although the cruel persecution of the Reformers by Beaton had no doubt much to do with his fearful and bloody end. This event did not help Henry in his scheme for uniting his son, the boy prince, with the baby queen, and he again attacked Scotland; taking ample vengeance for the rout at Ancrum Moor, by the destruction of the Scottish army at the battle of Pinkie, in 1547.

In the meantime Mary of Guise had not been idle. Her sympathies were with France and the Church of Rome. The Scots saw that the assistance of the French against the English was a matter of necessity, and the queen mother no doubt fostered this view. The Regent Arran was bought by a French title. The art and address of the queen were used, probably, as no woman of her time, except her own daughter, could use them. Finally a treaty of marriage was concluded between the infant Mary Stuart and the son of Henry II. of France, afterwards Francis II, and the child queen was placed under the guardianship of the French king and carried to France.

This stroke of policy enabled Mary of Guise to attempt

to obtain full powers as regent during the minority of her daughter; she cajoled, threatened, and eventually triumphed, in April, 1554. In short, it was simply a struggle between a clever, determined woman, and a careless, undecided, indolent man. Arran yielded in spite of some profane remarks on his meanness and want of courage, uttered by his brother, the Archbishop of St. Andrews.

The queen regent soon showed her capacity for government, and infused new vigour into the public administration. With the assistance of French troops she retook Haddington, and drove the English out of the garrisons held after the battle of Pinkie.

The great drawback of Mary of Guise in gaining full popularity with her subjects, was the fact that she was a Frenchwoman; and in the rising opinions of the Reformation there also lay another element of unpopularity, since she was devoted to the interests of the Church of Rome. The Scots, always jealous of foreign interference, grew more and more so as their rising liberties became more secure; hence they watched every action of Mary of Guise with suspicion.

In 1557 the marriage of the youthful Mary with the Dauphin Francis took place at Notre Dame, and by the treaty agreed to by the Scottish parliament, Francis was to be recognized as King of Scotland; all power being exercised in the names of Francis and Mary.

The death of Mary, Queen of England, and the accession of Elizabeth, gave a great impetus to the Reformation in England; and, as a matter of course, this had an important effect also on Scotland. John Knox had returned to his own country in 1555, and his zeal and eloquence had borne fruits in the party of the Congregation, as it was called, the leaders of which entered into a solemn league and covenant to establish the Word of God, and whilst maintaining the

H

doctrines of the Gospel of Christ, to put down all the super-stitious formalisms of the ancient church. This was prac-tically a declaration of open schism, heresy, and spiritual rebellion against the Roman clergy, which the latter received with scorn and indignation, but also with alarm.

Elizabeth of England saw the advantage which she might gain politically by assisting the recusant party, and no doubt secretly helped the Lords of the Congregation.

The commercial, middle, and lower classes, too, in Scot-land had become attached to the principles of the Reforma-tion from conviction, and Knox found little difficulty in persuading them by his preaching that England, their ancient enemy, had now become the leader in the great question of the time,—religious liberty; whilst France, the former ally of Scotland, was the enemy of Scotland in the interest of popery and prelacy.

Mary of Guise had acted with great judgment and tact in the early part of the regency, but as the progress of the Reformation became more and more decided, her caution seems to have been laid aside. The Princes of Guise, her brothers, had joined the league concluded between the Pope, the Emperor, and the King of Spain, for the rooting out of Protestantism, and through their influence the Queen Re-gent of Scotland became a party to the coalition. In the existing temper of the reformers, this was a fatal step.

In March, 1559, a convention of the clergy was held at Edinburgh, in which the Lords of the Congregation de-manded that no bishop should be elected without the assent of the nobles and gentry of the diocese, nor any parish priest appointed unless elected by the parishioners. Of course this was refused. The queen regent then issued a pro-clamation calling on all persons to attend mass and the con-fessional, ordering that all public prayers should be in Latin, and that all ministers not complying with the terms of the proclamation, should appear at Stirling to answer for their delinquency. They appeared, however, with Knox at their head, and bodies of armed retainers led by the nobles.

The queen regent, after some parley, was told that all the people required was to worship God after the dictates of their own conscience, with liberty to ministers of the Gospel. This brought out the hidden nature of the woman, and she promised that if the Congregation dispersed all would be well. They disbanded only to find themselves deceived, for the queen simply repeated the former summons, and on the failure of the clergy to appear, proclaimed them rebels.

This perfidy so enraged the Congregation that after a stern and stirring appeal from Knox, the fury of the people was let loose, and from that time the future of the Romish Church was settled in Scotland. Of course several attempts were made to compromise matters, in which the duplicity of Mary of Guise, the intolerance of the prelates who surrounded her, and the evil influence of her brothers, prevented all possibility of a peaceful solution of the difficulty; and a civil war resulted, in which France aided the queen regent and her partisans.

Of course the war was carried on in the midst of the most exasperated feelings on both sides. At first the Reformers feared for the result from the power of France being against them; but, eventually, Elizabeth of England strengthened them with an army under the Duke of Norfolk, and also assisted them with a fleet.

The death of Mary of Guise shortened the struggle. She died on 10th of June, 1560, her constitution, broken by anxiety, giving way under the pressure of events which were beyond her control.

On her death bed she expressed her sorrow for having allowed herself to be influenced to such an extent by advice which had produced such calamitous results, and brought the country into its then condition, and emphatically called upon those persons, representing both parties, by whom she was surrounded in her last moments, to support the authority of her daughter, Mary Queen of Scots, who, by her death, was left an orphan when she most needed a mother's care and counsel, for within a few months after, that daughter was left a widow by the death of her husband, Francis II. of France.

Commissioners met at Edinburgh, by whom it was arranged that the French troops should be withdrawn, and the validity of a treaty between Queen Elizabeth and the Congregation acknowledged. In this matter the diplomatic skill of Sir William Cecil, Elizabeth's minister, overreached the French commissioners. This treaty, however, the youthful sovereign, Mary, refused to ratify when presented to her at Paris, thus laying the foundation of serious difficulties in the future.

The authority from which the portrait was painted is a picture in the collection of his grace the Duke of Devonshire.

Mary Queen of Scots.

PROBABLY there is no individual in British history whose career has had so absorbing an interest for the great masses of the people as that of Mary Stuart, Queen of Scotland. Her youth, beauty, and accomplishments, the difficulties of the times in which she lived, and the varied factions with which her fate was from time to time mixed up, together with the romantic character of many of the incidents of her life, have all helped to make her memory a subject of peculiar interest, especially to her co-religionists of the Church of Rome.

Mary was the only daughter and third child of King James V. of Scotland, and Mary of Guise, and was born on 6th of December, 1642, eight days before the death of her father after the rout at Solway Moss. Her two infant brothers, Arthur and James, died some time before. Her mother, Mary of Guise, after the Earl of Arran had yielded up the position he first assumed, was regent of Scotland during the minority of the child queen, and had to contend with the revolutionary spirit of the Reformers, assisted as they were, unintentionally, by the intolerance of the adherents to the Church of Rome, as also by the direct encouragement they received from England.

Mary of Scotland, while quite an infant, was sent to France for education, and betrothed to the Dauphin

Francis, son of Henry II, and their engagement was concluded in a marriage, which took place at Notre Dame in 1557. In 1559 she became Queen of France as well as of Scotland, by the accession of her husband to the throne by the title of Francis II. He died in his eighteenth year, on 5th of December, 1560. She was thus left a widow at the early age of eighteen, her mother having died six months before.

Mary had been educated in probably the most brilliant, as it was also the most profligate court of Europe. Her beauty, accomplishments, winning manners, and generosity, had made her the centre of the society in which she had been brought up. Caressed, almost worshipped in France, the death of Francis compelled her immediate return to Scotland ; and to facilitate this, several members of each of the contending parties in the State were sent over from Edinburgh to invite her return to her native country. The representative of the Reformers was the Lord Jenner, afterwards the Regent Moray, a man of great ability and ambition.

She was received by all classes of her subjects with the greatest enthusiasm, and landed at Leith on 19th of August, 1561. Her education in the principles of the Church of Rome, her attachment to France and the brothers of her mother, the Guises, soon caused her to come into antagonism with the Parliament and the Lords of the Congregation, as representing the reforming spirit of the times, alike in Church and State. Anxious to conciliate all parties if possible, and especially to remain at peace with England, as, from the distracted condition of France, she could hope for no assistance from that country, Mary selected her principal advisers from the reforming party ; made Moray her chief minister, and did everything in her power to conciliate

Queen Elizabeth, who seems to have taken an unaccoutable dislike to her from some cause ; and certainly the treatment of Mary Stuart was characterized by a selfish and insincere policy, only to be equalled by that of Henry VIII.

Mary's subjects were naturally desirous that their youthful queen should marry, so that the succession to the throne might be secured, for few countries had suffered so much as Scotland from uncertainty on this point. Again, Mary was young and beautiful, and all who came within her influence felt her attractive and engaging manners. But then she was also the heir to the English throne after Elizabeth, and, therefore, desired to marry with the consent of that monarch. After several attempts to attain this object, in which she found herself cruelly deceived and betrayed, Mary resolved to act for herself; and having lost confidence in Moray and Lethington, as her ministers who had acted for her with Elizabeth, she reversed her policy, and seems to have broken away altogether from the Reforming party.

It was while under the influence of the contending feelings produced by injury and insult that Mary seems to have first met Henry Stuart, Lord Darnley, a handsome young nobleman, eldest son of the Earl of Lennox, and Lady Margaret Douglas, daughter of Queen Margaret and Angus, and consequently her cousin, who had been educated in England; and they were married in July, 1565, about four months after their first meeting. Darnley was then in his twenty-first year, and Mary in her twenty-third. He was handsome in person and attractive in manners, and appears not to have manifested the low propensities, or showed that deficiency of intellect which subsequently characterized him.

Suspected by Moray and Lethington of being a Roman Catholic, Darnley was an object of distrust to all the Reforming party, and Knox with his followers declared against the union. Elizabeth, too, showed her temper by ordering Lennox and Darnley, as British subjects, to repair to England. A convention of the Scottish nobility, however, approved the match, and in due course, as already stated, the marriage took place.

Surrounded by enemies, forsaken by the statesmen she had been in the habit of relying upon, the queen had to take the field and lead her armies against a powerful section of her subjects. Proclaiming Moray and his friends traitors, Mary drove them for protection to England, and though Elizabeth publicly repudiated them, she privately succoured them during their banishment.

Mary found, but too soon, that Darnley had no capacity for government, and that he was alike unworthy of her confidence or affection; nearly all her servants had betrayed her, her secretary, Maitland of Lethington, amongst the rest. This caused her unfortunately to avail herself of the services of David Rizzio, her foreign secretary. Rizzio seems to have presumed on this, and soon made many enemies. Darnley believed, or affected to believe, that Rizzio had displaced him in the queen's affections, and resolved to destroy him. On 9th of March, 1566, he was brutally assassinated in the presence of Mary by a party of nobles led by Darnley, or, at least, admitted by him to the queen's apartment. Rizzio claimed the protection of his royal mistress; but whilst one ruffian held a pistol to her breast, and another threatened to stab her,—a thirds truck the unfortunate secretary a blow with his dagger over the queen's shoulder, and he was eventually dragged from the apartment and nearly cut to pieces.

Mary was not likely to forgive Darnley such an outrage as this, and in due time punishment reached him, it is feared by the queen's connivance and consent, if not suggestion. At the time of this murder the queen was near her confinement, which made the circumstances even more atrocious than they would have been under other circumstances, since the agitation and excitement might have occasioned the death of both Mary and the expected heir.

With singular self-command she appeared to compromise the deed by outwardly, at least, accepting Darnley's excuses and explanation, if not denial of his consent to the murder, and restored some of the old ministers to power. After the birth of her son, James VI. of Scotland, afterwards James I. of England, Mary proceeded to organize a stronger government, and to repudiate Darnley's interference in public affairs. She reconciled the Earls of Bothwell and Moray. The latter, with Maitland, proposed a divorce from Darnley, but this was abandoned as likely to be injurious to the claims of her son ; but she had certainly become attached to Bothwell, thinking probably that, if circumstances favoured their future union, he would be a more powerful supporter of her government than the weak Darnley was ever likely to be. The latter was taken ill, having left the court, and absented himself from the baptism of the young prince, his son. His illness seemed to have roused the queen's sympathies, and she sent her own physician to attend him ; but a conspiracy had been entered into by certain nobles to get rid of him, Bothwell being the leader. Mary having been in attendance on Darnley in the evening of 9th of February, 1567, at the Kirk of Field, where he lay sick, left him, with every appearance of returned affection, to return to the palace. In the night the house was blown up by gunpowder, deposited, it is supposed, in the queen's bed-chamber, which was under that of the king ; and the dead body of the latter was afterwards found in the garden.

Bothwell was charged with the murder, and demanding a

trial, declared his innocence. The Earl of Lennox, father of Darnley, was to have appeared as accuser; but Bothwell appeared to take his trial surrounded by about four thousand friends and armed retainers, and as Lennox refused to attend as prosecutor under such circumstances, Bothwell was acquitted.

Unprincipled and profligate in more than an ordinary degree, even in those times, Bothwell took advantage of the queen's going from Edinburgh to Stirling attended, purposely it is supposed, by a small body guard, to seize upon and carry her with her suite to Dunbar Castle. Here, strange to say, she consented to marry him; and after hurrying through a process of divorce from his wife, this unholy union took place on 15th of May, 1567, within three months after the murder of Darnley.

All this had been done with the consent of a certain party of nobles, who now threw off all concealment, and resolved to separate Bothwell from Mary, and punish her as the assassin of Darnley. This ended in Bothwell being allowed to leave the queen unmolested, the latter being left a prisoner in the hands of her enemies, and conveyed to the strong castle of Loch Levin, and there kept a prisoner.

It was here she was compelled, on pain of death, as an accomplice in the murder of Darnley, to sign her abdication in favour of her son, to appoint Moray regent during his minority, and to appoint a temporary regency until Moray returned from France. The brutal Lord Lyndsay was the emissary of the nobles in this proceeding, and his treatment of the queen was an outrage on humanity.

The regent Moray assumed the conduct of affairs in the name of the boy king, James VI; but Mary managed to escape from Loch Levin, by the assistance of a youth, George Douglas, and riding to Niddy, and thence to

Hamilton, placed herself at the head of six thousand men. This force was ultimately intercepted by the regent before it could be reinforced, and the queen had to fly, and, it is said, rode from near Dunbarton to Dundrennan without drawing bridle, a distance of sixty miles. Finally, she had to seek refuge in England and appeal to Queen Elizabeth, who refused to receive her personally, but ordered her to be imprisoned; and Mary eventually remained in captivity for a period of nineteen years.

In 1572 an atrocious proposal was made by the English envoy to deliver Mary up to the Regent Mar and the Earl of Morton, so that she might be executed in Scotland for the supposed complicity with the murder of Darnley. Mar's death broke off this nefarious negotiation; but it was renewed two years after to the Regent Morton, who demanded money from Elizabeth, whose parsimony would not allow her to pay the price demanded. At length Mary was unjustly accused of having been a party to a plot against the life of the English queen. At first she declined to allow herself to be arraigned on any such a charge, but, unfortunately, afterwards consented, from a morbid idea that to refuse would be to appear to acknowledge her guilt. As a matter of course she was guilty of more than enough to give an excuse for destroying her; and after some affectation of delay, Elizabeth signed her death warrant, and Mary was executed at Fotheringhay Castle, on 7th of February, 1587, in her forty-fifth year.

The story of her execution has been so often told that it needs no repetition here. Her burial did not take place until 1st of August following her death. Her body was conveyed to Peterborough by torch-light on the night of 30th of July, and on the next day was interred on the south side of the choir of the Abbey Church, opposite the tomb of

RANCIS was the son of Henry II. of France and Catherine de Medicis. He succeeded his father in 1559, and was only in his seventeenth year. France was in a wretched state at the period of his accession. The exhaustion occasioned by a long war and the internal intrigues of various branches of the royal family, from the fact that he and his three younger brothers were the last male representatives of the house of Valois, had much to do with this condition of things. The introduction of the Reformed religion, too, had produced a convulsion in the society of the period, which acted and reacted upon the factions of the court; the two most formidable of which were then led by the Duke of Guise, and his opponent and rival, the Constable Montmorenci.

A mere youth like Francis could do little under such circumstances. His mother, the ambitious and unscrupulous Catherine de Medicis, whose cunning and duplicity had concealed her true character during the reign of her husband, became practically the ruler of France. Her hatred of the Huguenot or Protestant cause was manifested on all occasions; and aided by the Duke of Guise and his party, she carried on something like a war of extermination upon the unhappy people who were even suspected of any sympathy with the doctrines of the Reformed Church, which culminated in the celebrated massacre of St. Bartholomew's Day, under her second son, Charles IX.

Almost the only redeeming feature in the political history of the period, or in the character of the men of the time, is in that of the honest and good Michel de l'Hôpital, Chancellor of France. He laboured hard to promote the real welfare of all around him, sought to inculcate and, as far as his power lay, to enforce religious toleration, and for his efforts in the latter direction he was suspected of being a Protestant. He opposed Catherine on all occasions when he felt she was wrong; but his single-mindedness and patriotism probably shamed her into respect for his character.

Francis II. married Mary Stuart, afterwards so celebrated for her beauty and misfortunes as Mary Queen of Scots, in 1557. He died from an abscess in the head on 5th December, 1560, when nearly eighteen years of age, without issue.

The authority from which the portrait was executed is a picture by Janet in the collection at Hampton Court.

Lord Darnley.

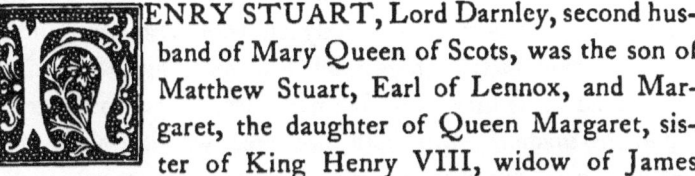ENRY STUART, Lord Darnley, second husband of Mary Queen of Scots, was the son of Matthew Stuart, Earl of Lennox, and Margaret, the daughter of Queen Margaret, sister of King Henry VIII, widow of James IV. of Scotland, and her second husband, Archibald Douglas, Earl of Angus. He was born and educated in England, as his father had been a refugee from the violence of the Hamilton faction at the court of King Henry VIII.

The marriage of Matthew Stuart, Earl of Lennox, with the niece of that monarch gave him an important position; and having settled down quietly to the usual pursuits of an English nobleman of the period, he found full compensation for his attainder and banishment from Scotland. Queen Elizabeth regarded him and his family with consideration; and, although she secretly desired to prevent Mary of Scotland marrying again, it is said that, amongst others whom she publicly pressed on Mary's attention, was Stuart's son, Henry Lord Darnley, at whose subsequent union with the unfortunate Scottish queen she became so furious and implacable.

During a visit which Lennox and his son paid to Scotland in February, 1565, Mary saw Darnley for the first time. He was then in his twenty-first year, a handsome and accomplished young nobleman—at least he was accomplished in all the external niceties of the conventional politeness of the time. Mary was at once greatly smitten with him, and it was soon evident that she intended to marry him; therefore the public announcement did not surprise her own court when she made it. Elizabeth, however, was terribly angry; not only with Mary, but with Darnley and his father, and ordered their return at once to England. The Scottish nobility were incited by the emissaries of Elizabeth to prevent the marriage; but this was of no avail, for it took place on 29th of July, 1565, and the day after the bride and bridegroom were proclaimed as Henry and Mary, King and Queen of Scotland.

Mary soon had reason to regret her haste. Fair as Darnley's person and outward manners were, they covered so many hideous faults that all reformation appeared hopeless. He was proud, insolent, and overbearing to those he considered beneath him; cruel and vindictive, he plotted with certain nobles to destroy David Rizzio, Mary's French secretary,—a man of mean birth, whom he had demeaned himself at first by making his friend and intimate; but of whom he became jealous after his neglect of the queen and devotion to vicious pursuits. Rizzio remonstrated with him and treated him with coldness, whilst showing great devotion to Mary. Darnley was deeply disappointed in obtaining no legal recognition from the Parliament of his title as king of Scotland; and certain nobles and friends of the Lennox family made this a matter of personal affront to themselves, which they proposed to revenge on Mary through Rizzio, whom they asserted had influenced the queen in this matter. A plot was planned, of which Darnley was undoubtedly fully cognizant, for the murder of the secretary; and on 9th of March, 1565, Rizzio was surprised by conspirators in the queen's apartments in Holyrood Palace, to which he had been in-

vited to supper, and there assassinated in the presence of
Queen Mary and Darnley.

Faithless, feeble, and irresolute, if not absolutely cowardly,
Darnley's conduct betrayed him to the queen, probably more
than any representation she might have received. Sometimes siding with Mary, at other times with the nobles in
arms against her authority; refusing to be present at the
baptism of his son, James VI, and adding insult to injury,
Henry Stuart acted with childish caprice, weakness, and
indecision. No doubt these annoyances and insults, togethre
with the conviction that Darnley was privy to, if not the
instigator of, Rizzio's murder, alienated any affection for
him which may have remained in Mary's heart. When to
this was added the attraction of a new favourite in the person of James Hepburn, Earl of Bothwell, whom Mary
eventually married for her third husband, there is motive
enough to cause her to devise the death of Darnley. After
residing at Stirling for a time almost alone, the latter sud-
denly went to Glasgow, from an apprehension that it was
intended to imprison him. On the way he was taken ill,
and although near death, Mary did not visit him. As soon
as he was better, however, and arrived at Glasgow, she
found him there and lavished upon him every possible attention, and finally persuaded him to remove to Edinburgh.
Carried there on a litter, but not to the palace, he was
lodged, under a pretence of better air and quietude, in a house
called Kirk of Field. Peevish, suspicious, and exacting as
he was, Mary attended to him assiduously, staying with him
almost constantly, until the evening of Sunday, 9th of February, 1567, when she left him late at night to be present
at a masque at the palace. In three hours after her
departure—two o'clock in the morning—the house was
blown up by gunpowder, and Darnley's lifeless body,

and also that of the servant who remained with him, were found at a little distance, bearing few or no marks of violence.

The authorities from which the portrait was painted are a picture by Lucas de Heere and an old engraving by Elstrack.

FINIS.

CHISWICK PRESS :— PRINTED BY WHITTINGHAM AND WILKINS, TOOKS COURT,
CHANCERY LANE.

www.ingramcontent.com/pod-product-compliance
Lightning Source LLC
Chambersburg PA
CBHW020226030726
47497CB00009B/2969